A CROWN OF MAPLES

Constitutional Monarchy in Canada

Canadä

Courtesy of the Government of Canada
Gracieuseté du gouvernement du Canada
publications.gc.ca

It is a privilege to serve you as Queen of Canada to the best of my ability, to play my part in the Canadian identity, to uphold Canadian traditions and heritage, to recognize Canadian excellence and achievement, and to seek to give a sense of continuity in these exciting, ever-changing times in which we are fortunate enough to live.

Queen Elizabeth II
Vancouver, British Columbia
October 2002

Her Majesty Queen Elizabeth II
Queen of Canada

wearing her Canadian insignia
as Sovereign of the Order of Canada
and the Order of Military Merit

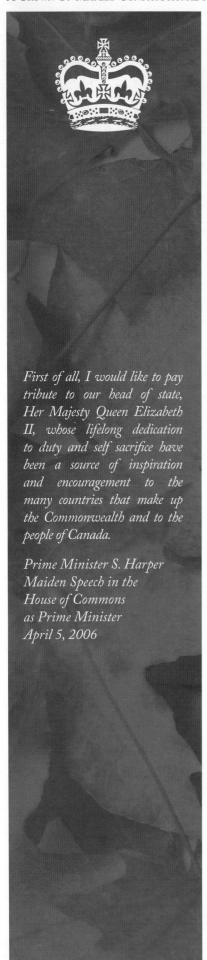

First of all, I would like to pay tribute to our head of state, Her Majesty Queen Elizabeth II, whose lifelong dedication to duty and self sacrifice have been a source of inspiration and encouragement to the many countries that make up the Commonwealth and to the people of Canada.

Prime Minister S. Harper
Maiden Speech in the
House of Commons
as Prime Minister
April 5, 2006

Her Majesty Queen Elizabeth II receives in audience the Honourable Stephen Harper, P.C., M.P. (then Leader of Her Majesty's Loyal Opposition) at Rideau Hall in Ottawa during the Golden Jubilee Visit (October 2002). On February 6, 2006, (the 54th anniversary of the accession to the Throne by Her Majesty as Queen of Canada), the Right Honourable Stephen Harper became Canada's 22nd Prime Minister.

PRIME MINISTER · PREMIER MINISTRE

Along with about eighty percent of Canadians, I have known no other Sovereign than Her Majesty Queen Elizabeth II. It was on February 6, 1952, less than three months following a coast to coast tour of Canada, that 25-year-old Princess Elizabeth became Queen upon the death of her father King George VI.

During the intervening and often tumultuous years since 1952, Elizabeth II has been steadfast in her commitment to this country and has executed her duties as Queen with a dignity, wisdom and dedication that is a model of service to all Canadians.

Canada has always had a monarch, since the time of King Henry VII of England and King Francis I of France. Today the Queen and her eleven representatives, the Governor General and the Lieutenant Governors, form the institution of the Canadian Crown – an institution that has, over time, been moulded to suit our own needs and character. At the heart of our system of government, the Canadian Crown is central to our uniquely Canadian identity. It is a reality that often works quietly behind the scenes, providing stability and continuity in a world often marked by upheaval and instability. The Crown commands allegiance but not conformity, making it an ideal embodiment of "unity in diversity."

A Crown of Maples is intended to make information on the Canadian Monarchy available to Canadians in an interesting and meaningful format. It is my hope that it will serve to foster an even greater awareness and appreciation of this Canadian institution and its ongoing importance to so many aspects of our country's daily life and the collective identity we all share and cherish.

The Rt. Hon. Stephen Harper, P.C., M.P.
Prime Minister of Canada

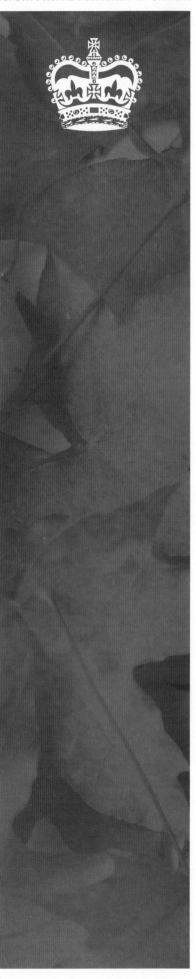

Table of Contents

I.   Introduction   1

II. The Canadian Crown – An Overview   5
     The Crown in Canadian History   6
     Constitutional Monarchy in Contemporary Canada   9

III. The Modern Reality of Constitutional Monarchy   15
     The Political Theory   16
     Canada's Constitutional Monarchy in Practice   16
     The Role of Constitutional Convention in
         Ensuring Responsible Government   18

IV. The Role and Powers of the Canadian Crown Today   23
     The Queen and Parliament/Legislatures   24
     Powers of the Crown   27
     The Queen as Head of State: Personifying the Country   30

V.   Canadian Representatives of the Crown   33
     The Governor General   34
     The Lieutenant Governors   37
     The Canadian Essence of Monarchy   38

VI. Comparison with Other Systems of Government   43

VII. The Visual Presence of the Canadian Crown   49
     The Crown as A Symbol of Statehood   50
     Canadian Honours of the Crown   51
     Ceremonial Occasions   54
     Royal Visits   54

VIII. Conclusion   59

The Royal Anthem – *God Save The Queen*   I

Appendices   III
Sovereigns of Canada   IV
Governors/Governors General of Canada   V

Photographic Credits   VIII

Glossary   XII

Acknowledgements   XVIII

Introduction

Chapter 1

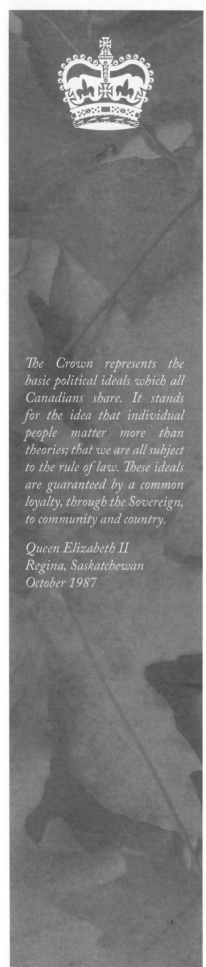

The Crown represents the basic political ideals which all Canadians share. It stands for the idea that individual people matter more than theories; that we are all subject to the rule of law. These ideals are guaranteed by a common loyalty, through the Sovereign, to community and country.

Queen Elizabeth II
Regina, Saskatchewan
October 1987

The Royal Arms of Canada (coat-of-arms) are the arms of Her Majesty The Queen in Right of Canada. A symbol of sovereignty, they are used on buildings, official seals, currency, passports, publications, proclamations and as rank badges of some members of the Canadian Forces.

Canada's maple leaf flag was proclaimed by Queen Elizabeth II to take effect on February 15, 1965 – the day it was first raised over Parliament Hill in Ottawa and in thousands of communities from coast to coast to coast.

Among the nations of the world, Canada is a young country. Yet, despite its youth, Canada has developed important traditions and institutions that have become an integral part of our national identity. One such institution is the Canadian Crown.

Throughout Canada's evolution into statehood, there has been no more visible and enduring institution than the Crown. Indeed, the roots of constitutional monarchy in Canada run deep into our soil. Initially established under the rule of the kings of France during the sixteenth, seventeenth and eighteenth centuries, Canada's monarchical institutions continued as a key element of government under the British Crown as a colony, during the eighteenth and nineteenth centuries. In 1867, the Fathers of Confederation (the thirty-six delegates from the British North American colonies pursuing the notion of political union) unanimously agreed that the new country would retain a monarchical system of government. The title "The Dominion of Canada" was deliberately chosen as a tribute to the very principles of monarchy that they wished to uphold. As a consequence of our evolution into statehood, Canada enjoys the status of a constitutional monarchy in its own right and remains today the largest in the world in terms of geographic size.

Her Majesty Queen Elizabeth II, Queen of Canada, is the sixth sovereign since Confederation in 1867. Although her father, King George VI, was specifically asked to govern Canada and respect its laws at his coronation in 1937, Queen Elizabeth was the first to be proclaimed independently Sovereign of Canada in 1953, following her accession to the Throne in 1952, and the first to bear the title Queen of Canada. Thirty years later, the patriation of the Constitution from the United Kingdom reaffirmed the central position of the Canadian Crown in the structure of our government.

When one hears the word "Crown," one often thinks of the actual crown worn by a king or queen. However, the Crown of Canada refers to something quite different. This booklet discusses the institution of the Crown, how it has evolved and grown with the country over hundreds of years as a uniquely Canadian institution, and the significant role it plays in the daily life of Canada today. It describes the people who represent the Crown and the relevance of its various functions.

A Crown of Maples is intended to provide a general examination of constitutional monarchy and explain why it remains an essential and relevant component of our national life in the twenty-first century. While outlining how our constitutional monarchy has evolved, it explains how the Canadian Crown continues to be one of our major national institutions and symbols, contributing to a sense of unity and pride among Canadians.

Princess Elizabeth (now Her Majesty Queen Elizabeth II) dances at Rideau Hall. Ottawa, Ontario. October 1951.

Queen Elizabeth II and The Duke of Edinburgh walk with Governor General Vincent Massey at Rideau Hall in Ottawa as an obliging "Duff" Massey carries Her Majesty's handbag. Ottawa, Ontario. October 1957.

Queen Elizabeth II and The Duke of Edinburgh with Her Majesty's Canadian Governor General, Prime Minister, Lieutenant Governors and Premiers on board HMY Britannia. Kingston, Ontario. July 1976.

Queen Elizabeth II speaks with members of the Doukhobor community of Veregin, Saskatchewan. October 1987.

Queen Elizabeth II reviews an R.C.M.P. guard of honour at Depot Division. Regina, Saskatchewan, May 2005.

From the moment when I first set foot on Canadian soil, the feeling of strangeness went, for I knew myself to be no only amongst friends, but amongst fellow countrymen.

> Queen Elizabeth II
> (Then Princess Elizabeth)
> 1951

The Canadian Crown
-An Overview

Chapter 2

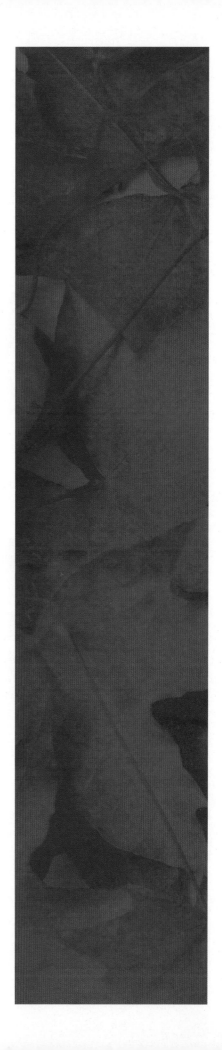

The Crown in Canadian History

The Crown in Canada was first established by the kings of France in the sixteenth century. Organized as a royal province of France, New France was administered by a governor — the personal representative of the king, who directed operations on behalf of the French Crown. Over the years, these governors, among them Samuel de Champlain, Frontenac and Vaudreuil, became closely identified with the early development of Canada.

During this period, kings and queens directed the affairs of their countries and, through governors, their overseas colonies. In every sense, the "Crown" reigned and ruled over the citizens in their daily lives. Its powers came from what was originally considered to be the divine right of kings, which gave the monarch almost absolute power to rule as he or she thought fit. It was with the *Treaty of Paris* of 1763 that the powers of the last absolute monarch to reign over Canada (King Louis XV of France) came to an end.

During the late eighteenth and early nineteenth centuries, Canada's monarchical institutions remained a pivotal aspect of its government. Following the American War of Independence, thousands of people who wished to remain loyal to the Crown relocated to the British North American colonies (Canada). This served to further deepen the attachment between Crown and people. British governors such as James Murray, Sir Guy Carleton (Lord Dorchester), and the Earl of Elgin were appointed as representatives of the Crown for the colonies and played an integral role in our evolution to statehood.

The Sovereign Council meeting during the Ancient Regime (painting by Charles Huot)

The Arms of Royalist France

At the same time, kings and queens had slowly begun to use advisers to assist them with their duties as rulers. With the accession to the Throne of Great Britain of King George I in 1714, sovereigns allowed these advisers, who often were elected politicians, to rule for them. (Queen Anne, who reigned from 1702 to 1714, was the last monarch to actually preside over the cabinet of British Ministers of the Crown.) This development flowed from the campaign for responsible government — the struggle to make elected governments responsible to the representatives duly voted in by the

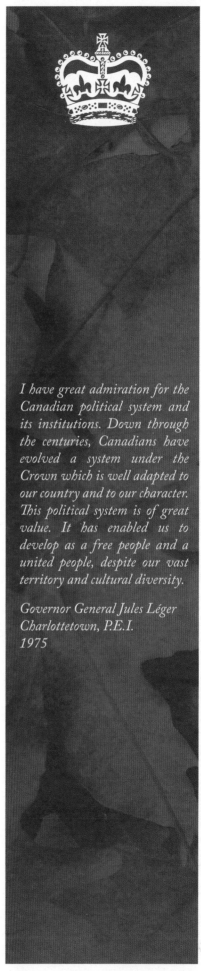

King Edward I of England, who reigned from 1272 to 1307, was a reformer who summoned a comprehensive assembly and emphasized the role of Parliament and the Common Law. The first Statute of Westminster (1275) codified many laws that originated with Magna Carta. Edward's "Model Parliament" contained representatives of all estates (barons, clergy, knights, townspeople) and was the foundation of the English Parliament at Westminster.

people. Colonial governments became accountable to the elected legislative assembly as they began to perform many Crown duties earlier carried out by the Sovereign or governor. This arrangement, with the executive of an elected government fulfilling the duties and exercising the powers of the Monarch, is known as a system of responsible government under a constitutional monarchy.

The first responsible government overseas in the British Empire was established in Nova Scotia in 1848. Over the next seven years, Prince Edward Island (1851), New Brunswick (1854), and Newfoundland (1855) followed Nova Scotia's example.

King Louis IX of France, who reigned from 1226 to 1270, rendered justice to his subjects using councillors in order to ensure good judgements. These councillors were the precursors of the Parliament of Paris that was to formalize rulings in the form of the Civil Code (the general law containing all of the basic provisions that govern life in society) as executed in both France and New France.

The colonies that united and formed the Dominion of Canada in 1867 had already enjoyed a long and uninterrupted association with the Crown. While the powers exercised by the Sovereign changed as Canada evolved into statehood, the link between Crown and people remained strong. The late Senator Eugene Forsey, one of Canada's leading constitutional experts, reminded us through his extensive writings that Canada had never had a republican form of government; by deliberate choice, Canada had been a monarchy from its earliest days.

At the Québec Conference in 1864, the political leaders of the day who became known as the Fathers of Confederation were unanimous in stating that the new country should remain a constitutional monarchy. Canada thus did not have monarchy forced upon it. Rather, the Fathers of Confederation understood the key role that the Crown played — and would continue to play — in bringing the colonies together as one country. United not by revolution but by peaceful consensus, the new country was based on a process of political evolution that flowed from the *Magna Carta* in England in 1215 and the lifelong crusade for social justice of Saint Louis (King Louis IX of France), and spanned hundreds of years of struggle for liberty and freedom. By insisting on retaining constitutional monarchy for Canada, the Fathers were continuing the long and proud tradition of

I have great admiration for the Canadian political system and its institutions. Down through the centuries, Canadians have evolved a system under the Crown which is well adapted to our country and to our character. This political system is of great value. It has enabled us to develop as a free people and a united people, despite our vast territory and cultural diversity.

*Governor General Jules Léger
Charlottetown, P.E.I.
1975*

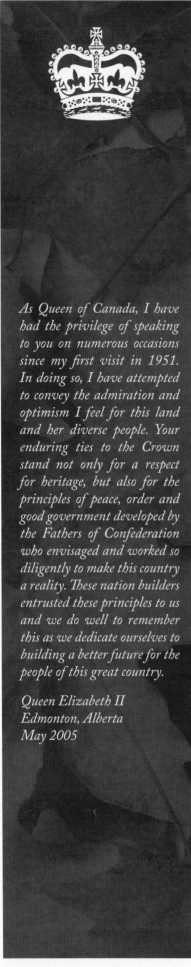

The Fathers of Confederation at the Québec City conference of 1864 (painting by Robert Harris)

maintaining an institution that was relevant, valued, and traced its very roots to the beginnings of Canada itself

In 1867, parliamentary democracy and responsible government under the Crown became cherished values in the new federal system. In this way, the Government of Canada continued to be vested in the Sovereign, who would continue to "reign" over Canada and serve as head of State. The Ministers of the Crown, with the Prime Minister as the head of Government, would be responsible to the people through the elected house of assembly — the House of Commons — and would rule "in trust" for Her Majesty Queen Victoria.

Constitutional monarchy respresented the continuation of democratic principles of government achieved over many years. Yet the Crown would evolve in the years following 1867 and become a uniquely Canadian institution — an enduring monarchy in a parliamentary democracy within a new federation.

The arms of the City of Québec, based on the proposal of Count Frontenac to the Minister of Colonies in October 1673 but never granted by French authorities. Two hundred and ninety five years later (1988), these arms were the first to be granted by the newly created Canadian Heraldic Authority.

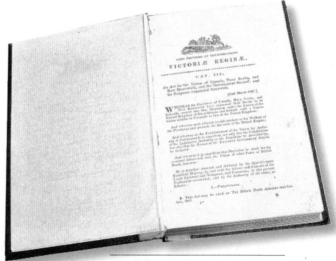

The British North America Act, 1867 (The Constitution Act, 1867)

Constitutional Monarchy in Contemporary Canada

Fifty years after Confederation, Canada attained a true and lasting sense of statehood at the Battle of Vimy Ridge in 1917 and actively worked for its autonomy to be acknowledged both at home and on the international stage. Building on resolutions passed at the Imperial Conferences of 1926 and 1930, Canada and the other Dominions of the then British Empire sought formal recognition of their autonomy from the United Kingdom. This was to find expresssion through the granting of equal legislative status for all the self-governing Dominions. An act of the British Parliament, the *Statute of Westminster, 1931*, affirmed the autonomy of Canada and the other countries of the Empire such as Australia and New Zealand. In addition, it recognized the virtual independence that had existed in principle since the First World War and the *Treaty of Versailles* that followed. Beyond marking a truly significant milestone in our evolution as an independent country, the *Statute of Westminister, 1931*, can be seen, in many ways, as the foundation or charter of the present-day Commonwealth. Moreover, with the passage of this law, the Canadian Crown became something that was Canada's own.

In December 1931, the *Statute of Westminster* clarified the relationship between the United Kingdom and its former colonies by formalizing full legal independence and legislative autonomy for the Realms — countries that recognized the Sovereign as their Head of State. Canada became an autonomous and equal member within the then Empire (now the Commonwealth) with the Crown as the common link.

On the death of King George VI in February 1952, his daughter Princess Elizabeth immediately succeeded to the Throne as Queen. When the coronation ceremony took place the following year, Her Majesty was proclaimed in Canada with the following

Her Excellency Michaëlle Jean, Governor General of Canada, celebrates National Aboriginal Day with residents of Fort Simpson, Northwest Territories. June 21, 2006.

Her Majesty Queen Elizabeth II greets Canadian veterans and youth at the ceremony commemorating the ninetieth anniversary of the Battle of Vimy Ridge. Vimy Ridge, France. April 9, 2007.

His Honour Pierre Duchesne, Lieutenant Governor of Quebec (centre), is congratulated following his swearing in as the twenty-eighth Lieutenant Governor of the province since Confederation. Québec City, Quebec. June 7, 2007.

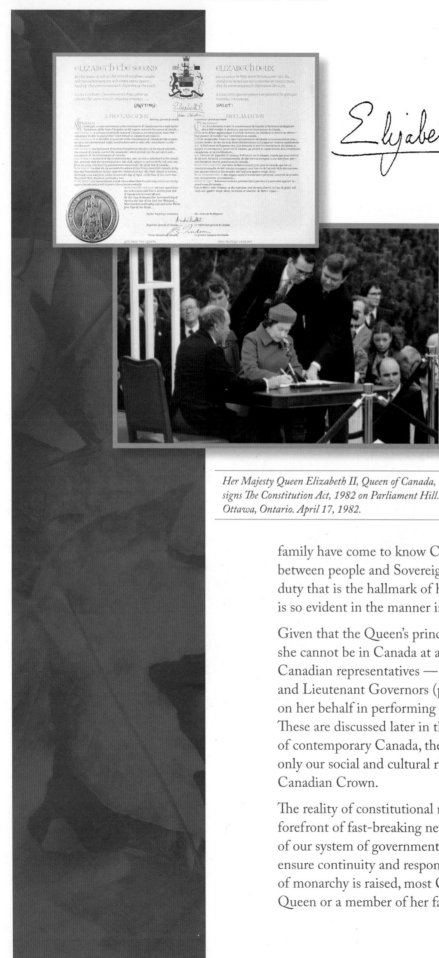

Her Majesty Queen Elizabeth II, Queen of Canada, signs The Constitution Act, 1982 on Parliament Hill. Ottawa, Ontario. April 17, 1982.

words: "By the Grace of God, of the United Kingdom, Canada and Her other Realms and Territories Queen, Head of the Commonwealth, Defender of the Faith." The proclamation reaffirmed the newly crowned monarch's position as Queen of Canada, a role totally independent from that as Queen of the United Kingdom and the other Commonwealth Realms.

Since her first tour of Canada in 1951 before ascending the Throne, Queen Elizabeth has been a frequent visitor to all regions of Canada. Her Majesty has taken an abiding interest in Canada and the issues that concern us as a country. The Queen and her family have come to know Canada well and a strong bond of affection between people and Sovereign has been reinforced by the dedication to duty that is the hallmark of her personal commitment to her role that is so evident in the manner in which she fulfills it.

Given that the Queen's principal residence is in the United Kingdom, she cannot be in Canada at all times. It is for this reason that her Canadian representatives — the Governor General (federally) and Lieutenant Governors (provincially) — are appointed and act on her behalf in performing certain duties and responsibilities. These are discussed later in this booklet. In reflecting the true face of contemporary Canada, these eleven individuals highlight not only our social and cultural richness, but also the uniqueness of the Canadian Crown.

The reality of constitutional monarchy is that, while not always at the forefront of fast-breaking news, the Crown forms a fundamental part of our system of government. It serves quietly behind the scenes to ensure continuity and responsibility of government. When the subject of monarchy is raised, most Canadians will think of a royal visit by the Queen or a member of her family, the reading of the *Speech from the*

Throne by the Governor General, or perhaps a Lieutenant Governor's visit to a community or the presentation of an award to a deserving individual. This visible presence of monarchy is itself quite important. It reminds us that the Crown and its representatives are living symbols of our collective freedoms and institutions and that they function as guardians of our democratic system of government. Further, we will see in subsequent pages that there are varied and important responsibilities that must be fulfilled and duties that must be performed on a daily basis.

On February 15, 1965, following a Royal Proclamation signed by Her Majesty The Queen, Canada's red and white maple leaf flag was raised for the first time on Parliament Hill in Ottawa. Thousands of Canadians were present for this historic moment, including the Queen's national representative, Governor General Georges P. Vanier, Her Canadian Prime Minister, the Rt. Hon. Lester B. Pearson, and the Leader of Her Majesty's Loyal Opposition, the Rt. Hon. John Diefenbaker.

One of the final acts of Canadian nation building was the patriation of our Constitution from the United Kingdom. This milestone was formalized by the signing of a Royal Proclamation by Her Majesty The Queen, as Queen of Canada, on Parliament Hill on April 17, 1982.

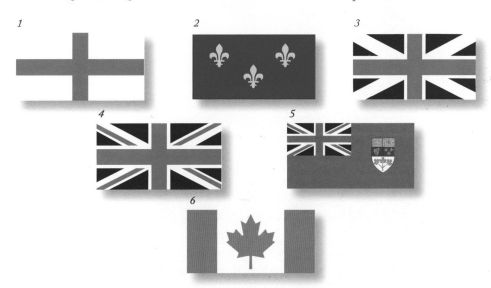

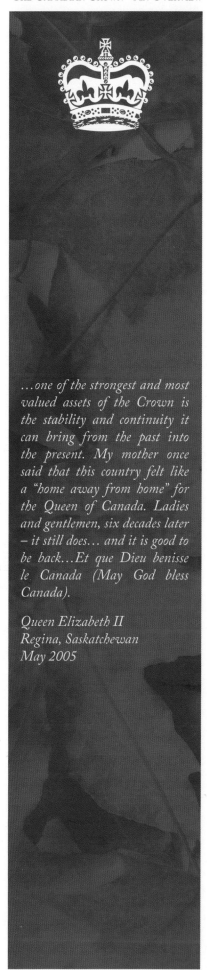

...one of the strongest and most valued assets of the Crown is the stability and continuity it can bring from the past into the present. My mother once said that this country felt like a "home away from home" for the Queen of Canada. Ladies and gentlemen, six decades later – it still does... and it is good to be back...Et que Dieu benisse le Canada (May God bless Canada).

*Queen Elizabeth II
Regina, Saskatchewan
May 2005*

1. St. George's Cross - the flag of 15th century England carried by John Cabot (1497);

2. Fleur-de-lis - a variation of this flag of Royalist France carried by Jacques Cartier (1534) and used until 1763;

3. Royal Union Flag - the flag of the British North American colonies (1763-1800);

4. Royal Union Flag (Union Jack) - the flag of the British North American colonies with the addition of the Cross of St. Patrick (post 1800). In December 1964, Parliament approved the continued use of the Union Flag as a symbol of Canada's membership in the Commonwealth and of her allegiance to the Crown;

5. Canadian Red Ensign - while several earlier versions existed from 1870, this design was created and approved in 1924 and was flown until the adoption of Canada's national flag in 1965;

6. The National Flag of Canada - proclaimed by Queen Elizabeth II to take effect on February 15, 1965.

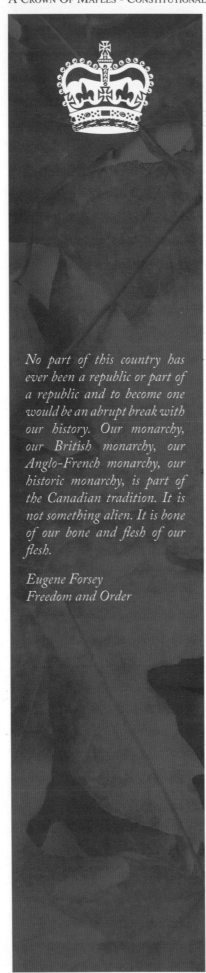

No part of this country has ever been a republic or part of a republic and to become one would be an abrupt break with our history. Our monarchy, our British monarchy, our Anglo-French monarchy, our historic monarchy, is part of the Canadian tradition. It is not something alien. It is bone of our bone and flesh of our flesh.

Eugene Forsey
Freedom and Order

Far from diminishing the role or power of the Crown, patriation reaffirmed and entrenched the position of constitutional monarchy: any amendments affecting the position of the Queen or her representatives now require the concurrence of the Parliament of Canada and all ten provincial legislatures.

As Canadians move ahead into the twenty-first century with confidence and pride, some may think that monarchy is an ancient institution that has little or no place in a modern, technologically-advanced society like ours. Such a perception is far from accurate. Beyond ceremonial occasions, which occur in the life of every nation, the Crown continues to possess very tangible powers that can and must be exercised, however seldom, in extraordinary situations. In the following section, we look at how both the political theory and actual practice of constitutional monarchy work in an independent Canada.

Queen Elizabeth II at the University of British Columbia during her Golden Jubilee Visit. Vancouver, British Columbia. October 2002.

Her Majesty Queen Elizabeth II presents a stone tablet to the First Nations University of Canada. Regina, Saskatchewan. May 17, 2005.

This stone was taken from the grounds of Balmoral Castle in the Highlands of Scotland – a place dear to my great great grandmother, Queen Victoria. It symbolizes the foundation of the rights of First Nations peoples reflected in treaties signed with the Crown during her reign. Bearing the cypher of Queen Victoria as well as my own, this stone is presented to the First Nations University of Canada in the hope that it will serve as a reminder of the special relationship between the Sovereign and all First Nations people.

Queen Elizabeth II
Regina, Saskatchewan
May 17, 2005

The Modern Reality of Constitutional Monarchy

Chapter 3

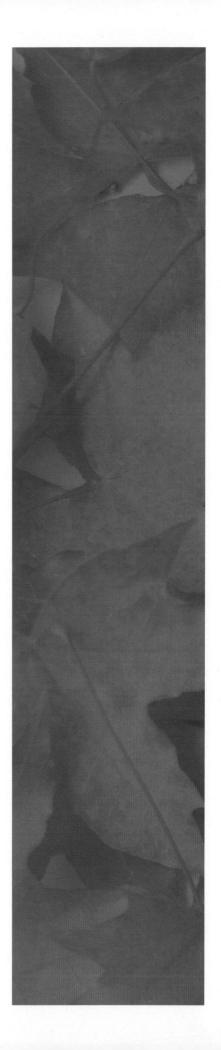

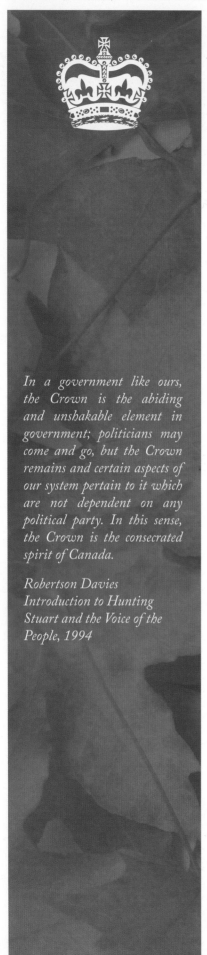

In a government like ours, the Crown is the abiding and unshakable element in government; politicians may come and go, but the Crown remains and certain aspects of our system pertain to it which are not dependent on any political party. In this sense, the Crown is the consecrated spirit of Canada.

Robertson Davies
Introduction to Hunting Stuart and the Voice of the People, 1994

The Great Seal of Canada bears the effigy of Queen Elizabeth II sitting on the coronation chair. The seal is affixed to many official documents and is a symbol of Canadian sovereignty. A document carrying the Great Seal is seen as having been sealed with the authority of the Queen of Canada.

The Political Theory

In a constitutional monarchy such as Canada's, power does not rest with any one person. Rather, power lies within an institution that functions to safeguard it on behalf of all its citizens. That institution is the Crown.

In political terms, Canada is both a federal state and a parliamentary democracy. It is also a constitutional monarchy with a responsible system of government. Responsible governments are elected by the people and are accountable to their duly elected representatives. A cornerstone of our system lies in the principle that governments use power but never possess it; power remains vested in the Crown and is only "entrusted" to governments to use on behalf of the people. In this way, power resides with a non-partisan institution that is above the political give and take inherent in the daily operations of government in every democracy.

Simply stated, in Canada as a constitutional monarchy, the government rules while the Crown reigns.

Canada's Constitutional Monarchy in Practice

Why is it necessary to deal with power in this way and, in the process, make this distinction between ruling and reigning? How does the Crown, by having power placed in it, serve to safeguard our rights and freedoms in a democratic system of government?

Part of the answer lies in the fact that governments are often tempted to view themselves as the very embodiment of the state: their long-term goal, after all, is to remain in office. However, the institution of the Crown reminds them that the source of power rests elsewhere and is only entrusted to them for a limited period of time. The Crown and its representatives remain vigilant in reinforcing the fact that our governments are the servants of the people and not the reverse.

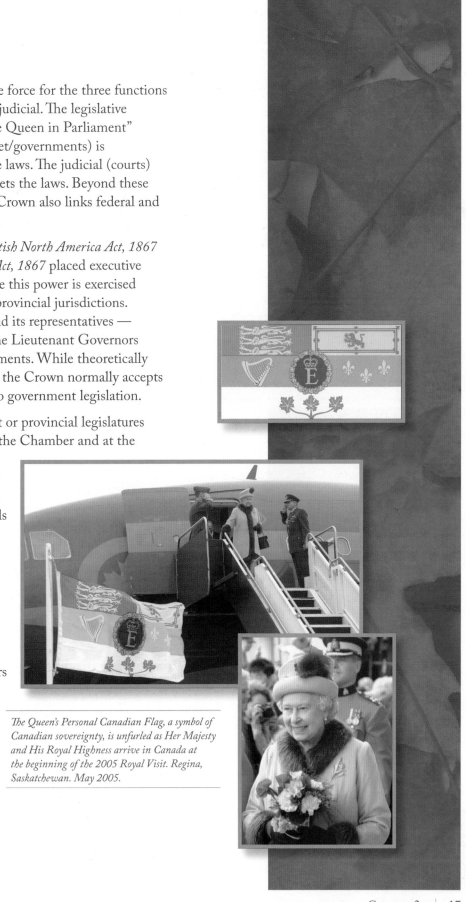

As an institution, the Crown is a cohesive force for the three functions of government: legislative, executive and judicial. The legislative function (Parliament/Legislature) is "The Queen in Parliament" and enacts the laws. The executive (cabinet/governments) is "The Queen in Council" and executes the laws. The judicial (courts) is "The Queen on the Bench" and interprets the laws. Beyond these important functions of government, the Crown also links federal and provincial governments in a federal state.

Canada's original Constitution is the *British North America Act, 1867* that was later renamed the *Constitution Act, 1867* placed executive power in the Crown. However, in practice this power is exercised by governments in both the federal and provincial jurisdictions. In exercising these powers, the Crown and its representatives — the Queen, the Governor General and the Lieutenant Governors — are advised by their respective governments. While theoretically free to refuse such advice, by convention, the Crown normally accepts and provides the final legitimizing step to government legislation.

Bills placed before the federal Parliament or provincial legislatures are enacted into law following debate in the Chamber and at the appropriate committees. It is only with the approval of the Governor General or Lieutenant Governor or, in their absence a designated administrator, that such bills receive Royal Assent and become law.

Although the Crown and its representatives are almost always bound to accept the advice offered by their governments, there are occasional circumstances whereby discretionary powers that are officially referred to as "reserve powers" can be used. Such powers are seldom used, given the strength of our system of government within the framework of our constitutional monarchy. All the same, the fact that they are rarely exercised does not mean they do not exist. We will see later how and when such powers have been exercised by the Crown in Canada.

The Queen's Personal Canadian Flag, a symbol of Canadian sovereignty, is unfurled as Her Majesty and His Royal Highness arrive in Canada at the beginning of the 2005 Royal Visit. Regina, Saskatchewan. May 2005.

Her Honour Barbara Hagerman, Lieutenant Governor of Prince Edward Island, reads the Speech from the Throne in historic Province House. Charlottetown, Prince Edward Island. November 2006.

In the day-to-day operation of government, the use of terms such as "The Queen's Privy Council for Canada," "Her Majesty's Government" and "the Leader of Her Majesty's Loyal Opposition" serves to reinforce the point that basic authority and legitimacy of government flow from the Crown on behalf of the people.

Governor General Michaëlle Jean grants Royal Assent in the Senate Chamber, witnessed by Prime Minister Stephen Harper. December 2006.

The Role of Constitutional Convention in Ensuring Responsible Government

As we have seen, the system of government of our country puts abstract political theory into practice through successful, well-established customs called "political conventions," in both federal and provincial jurisdictions.

Canada has a constitution comprising three elements: the written Constitution - *the Constitution Acts, 1867 to 1982)*; legislation, such as the *Royal Proclamation, 1763*, the *Manitoba Act*, the *Saskatchewan Act*, the *Alberta Act* and the *Statute of Westminster, 1931*); and the unwritten Constitution, which includes Common Law and constitutional conventions. To understand conventions, we must first recognize that many aspects of our system of government are not even mentioned in our Constitution. For example, there is no reference to the powers of the Crown to dissolve Parliament and call a general election, which are normally exercised on the advice of the Prime Minister. Indeed, the Constitution did not even make reference to the Prime Minister, or provincial Premiers or federal/provincial cabinets, until it was patriated in 1982. What could possibly explain important "omissions" such as these?

Under our parliamentary system of government, much of the functioning of government is based on conventions as opposed to

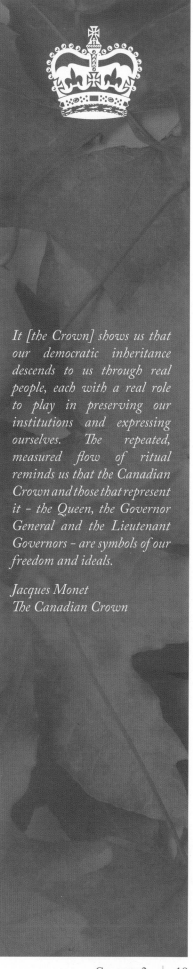

constitutional law. These conventions are neither found in law, nor are they part of the law — whether written or statute law or unwritten Common Law. Rather, they are established practices that have evolved over time. The principle of responsible government, which is a critical component of our democratic system, is itself a convention. It is the Crown that remains the guardian of the principles of responsible government in that it holds the power to dismiss a government which, in breach of constitutional conventions, would attempt to remain in office after it had lost the confidence of the elected House.

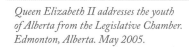

Queen Elizabeth II addresses the youth of Alberta from the Legislative Chamber. Edmonton, Alberta. May 2005.

It [the Crown] shows us that our democratic inheritance descends to us through real people, each with a real role to play in preserving our institutions and expressing ourselves. The repeated, measured flow of ritual reminds us that the Canadian Crown and those that represent it - the Queen, the Governor General and the Lieutenant Governors - are symbols of our freedom and ideals.

Jacques Monet
The Canadian Crown

Governor General Michaëlle Jean and a recipient (Major Chilton-Mackay) of the Order of Military Merit, at an investiture ceremony. Rideau Hall. Ottawa, Ontario. May 2007.

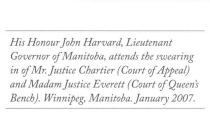

His Honour John Harvard, Lieutenant Governor of Manitoba, attends the swearing in of Mr. Justice Chartier (Court of Appeal) and Madam Justice Everett (Court of Queen's Bench). Winnipeg, Manitoba. January 2007.

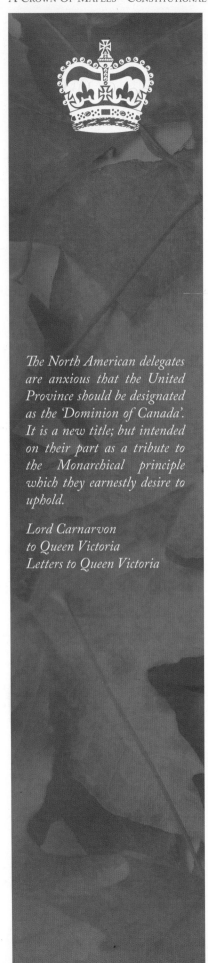

The North American delegates are anxious that the United Province should be designated as the 'Dominion of Canada'. It is a new title; but intended on their part as a tribute to the Monarchical principle which they earnestly desire to uphold.

Lord Carnarvon to Queen Victoria Letters to Queen Victoria

The following two chapters explain the role and actual powers of the Crown, both statutory, those written in law, and prerogative powers governed by constitutional convention. However, to fully appreciate the important role of the Sovereign and her representatives, we must begin with the understanding that while these powers are few, they exist to be used if and when necessary. Without them, the operation of government, indeed our democratic system, could be seriously hampered. In this way, the Crown can be seen as a safeguard in ensuring that cherished principles of democracy are respected on behalf of all Canadians.

Queen Elizabeth II greets young Canadians during a visit to the RCMP Musical Ride Equitation Centre. Ottawa, Ontario. October 2002.

His Honour Gordon Barnhart, Lieutenant Governor of Saskatchewan, and Her Honour Naomi Barnhart celebrate National Flag of Canada Day with students from Walker Elementary School and mascot "Salut". Regina, Saskatchewan. February 15, 2007.

Governor General Michaëlle Jean speaks with five-year- old champion Jeevan Basra at a reception for the Children's Miracle Network Champion Children. Rideau Hall. Ottawa, Ontario. March 2007.

Her Majesty Queen Elizabeth II and His Royal Highness The Duke of Edinburgh visit RCMP Depot Division in Regina, Saskatchewan to pay tribute to the fallen, shortly after the tragic loss of four officers at Meyerthorpe, Alberta. May 19, 2005.

CST. A. F. O. GORDON
CST. L. N. JOHNSTON
CST. B. W. MYROL
CST. P. C. SCHIEMANN

May I take this opportunity to salute an exceptional group of people who have been with me on all my visits – the Royal Canadian Mounted Police. While the scarlet tunic of the Mountie has come to symbolize Canada throughout the world, it is the Mountie's dedication to service and honour that embodies the spirit of so may of those who have built the nation as we know it today.

> *Queen Elizabeth II*
> *Arrival to Canada Ceremony*
> *Regina, Saskatchewan*
> *May 18, 2005*

The Role and Powers of the Canadian Crown Today

Chapter 4

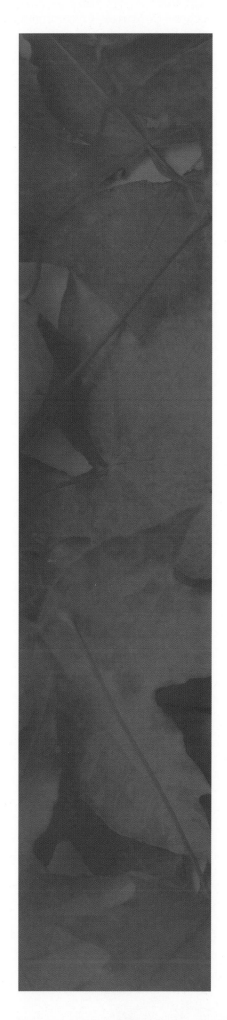

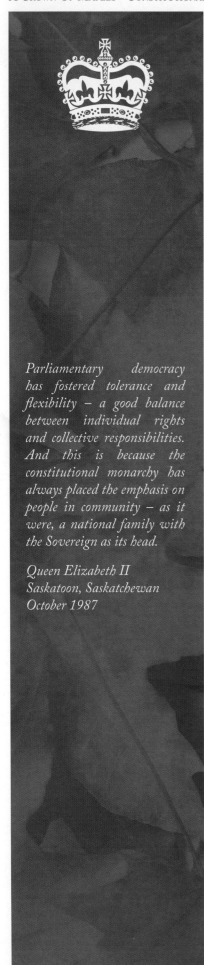

Parliamentary democracy has fostered tolerance and flexibility – a good balance between individual rights and collective responsibilities. And this is because the constitutional monarchy has always placed the emphasis on people in community – as it were, a national family with the Sovereign as its head.

Queen Elizabeth II
Saskatoon, Saskatchewan
October 1987

The Parliament Buildings, Ottawa, Ontario – seat of the federal Parliament of Canada

The Queen and Parliament/Legislatures

In our parliamentary system of government, the executive branch — the Prime Minister/Premier and cabinet — is responsible to the legislative branch — House of Commons/legislature — and, by extension, to the people. Whether the government is federal or provincial, authority to govern ultimately flows from the Crown.

The Parliament of Canada consists of the Queen, the Senate and the House of Commons. In the provinces, legislatures consist of the Lieutenant Governor and the elected assembly. The Governor General and Lieutenant Governors, whose duties are discussed in greater detail in the following chapter, represent the Queen and exercise her responsibilities on behalf of the people.

We are all familiar with the pomp and circumstance involved in the opening of Parliament and the reading of the *Speech from the Throne*, which outlines the government's legislative plans for the next parliamentary session. Beyond the obvious pageantry of the moment, what precise role does the Crown play in the functioning of government?

It is the Queen's representative, upon advice from the Prime Minister or Premier, who appoints individuals to the cabinet, making them "Ministers of the Crown." Just as the Prime Minister and Premiers are the Queen's "first ministers," so too are cabinet members advisers to the Crown. Through its right to advise and to be advised, the Crown exerts what is perhaps its principal influence. Although they almost always accept the advice of ministers, the representatives of the Crown do have the right and, indeed, the duty to have their views taken into account.

The nineteenth-century British constitutional expert, Walter Bagehot, stated that the three rights of the Sovereign were the rights to be consulted, to encourage and to warn. Former and current Prime Ministers and Premiers in Canada have found that their meetings

The Mace of the House of Commons

The House of Commons Chamber – the lower house of the Canadian Parliament

with the Queen's representative were invaluable in assisting them in the heavy responsibility of governing. The Crown's non-partisan and appropriately neutral position serves to reinforce stability in a discreet, behind-the-scenes manner.

It is in the name of the Queen that her representatives call Parliament or legislatures into session and dissolve it at the end of each respective term. When visiting the House of Commons in Ottawa or provincial/territorial legislatures, you can see a mace or staff resting in the chamber while it is in session. Bearing a Crown, the mace is a symbol of the legitimate right of the legislature to sit under authority of the Crown. As previously noted, all bills of the federal parliament and provincial legislatures must receive Royal Assent from the Crown. By introducing bills with the words "Her Majesty, by and with the advice and consent of...", we are reminded that it is the Sovereign, not the government, who is the ultimate guardian of our parliamentary democracy.

The granting of Royal Assent is itself another convention exercised by the Crown. While assent is rarely withheld, there are approximately ninety instances in Canadian history, all within provincial jurisdictions, when assent was not granted — the last occurring in Prince Edward Island in 1945. Royal Assent has not been withheld in the federal jurisdiction since Confederation; indeed, the last such case took place in the United Kingdom in 1707. The power of reservation — the referral of a provincial bill by a Lieutenant Governor to the Governor General for review — last occurred with regard to a bill in Saskatchewan in 1961. As confirmed by the passage of time, this power could be considered by some to be obsolete.

The Senate Chamber – the upper house of the Canadian Parliament

Another of the Crown's prerogative powers is to ensure there is always a first minister — specifically, a Prime Minister or Premier. After a general election, the incumbent Prime Minister/Premier makes clear

Queen Elizabeth II reads the Speech from the Throne in the Senate Chamber, October 14, 1957 and October 18, 1977.

I dedicate myself anew to the people and the nation I am proud to serve.

*Queen Elizabeth II
Speech from the Throne
Ottawa, Ontario
October 1977*

his/her intention to resign from office as soon as a replacement has been appointed. The resignation is accepted by the Crown's representative once the Governor General or Lieutenant Governor has called upon the party leader holding a majority of seats in Parliament or legislature to form a government. The process seems straightforward. On the other hand, what happens when there is no majority — a situation that has actually occurred frequently in Canadian political history?

If no political party holds a majority, the Governor General or Lieutenant Governor calls on a member who he/she believes, upon careful reflection, might be able to command majority support. Although the incumbent Prime Minister or Premier has the initiative by constitutional convention, the final decision rests with the representative of the Crown.

A reality of "minority governments" is that their life is often quite short. If the government is defeated in the House of Commons or legislature on a vote of non-confidence, the Crown's representative must either dissolve Parliament by calling an election or call on yet another member to attempt to form a government that would enjoy majority support. Far from existing only in political theory, this prerogative power has indeed been exercised in Canada — for example, in Ontario in 1985.

Since Confederation, Prime Ministers most commonly resign as a result of a defeat at a general election. Twelve Prime Ministers have been defeated and subsequently resigned, for a total of thirteen times, having applied to Mackenzie King on two separate occasions. However, the office can also be vacated due to other factors, such as resignation based on personal reasons, death or incapacitation. Since 1867, there have been eight such cases of prime ministerial "personal resignations," thereby making way for a new party leader who was then sworn in as Prime Minister. Among examples were the resignations

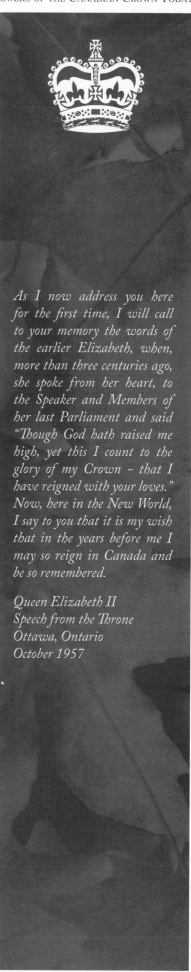

of Prime Minister Chrétien in December 2003, who was succeeded by Paul Martin, and Prime Minister Mulroney in June 1993, who was succeeded by Kim Campbell. A personal resignation in a provincial jurisdiction took place in Alberta in December 2006 when Premier Ralph Klein resigned and was succeeded by Ed Stelmach.

Once again, it is the responsibility of the Crown to ensure there is a new first minister and a government in office. Often, the choice is obvious; sometimes it is not. It falls to the Crown's representative to make sure that the interests of the people and the democratic system of government are respected and protected at all times.

Powers of the Crown

Besides its prerogative powers, the Crown also has statutory powers as stated in law. For example, our Constitution lists specific authorities for the Queen and the Governor General, including the appointment of senators, judges of certain courts, Lieutenant Governors in the provinces, and members of the Queen's Privy Council for Canada. Lieutenant Governors have the power to appoint members of the provincial Executive Council or Cabinet.

Although the Governor General and Lieutenant Governors are, in theory, free to refuse the advice of the Privy Council or Executive Council, in practice, they almost never do. Nevertheless, circumstances may give rise to a grave difference of opinion between the Crown's representatives and their advisors. Here, a special and generally less known area of the prerogative power, known as "reserve powers," comes into play.

These powers are a form of authority that can be used by the Crown's representatives only in exceptional or extenuating circumstances. Usually, the Queen's representatives entrust the use of the Crown's historical right of political power to elected politicians. As long as the government has the support of a majority of members in the House of

As I now address you here for the first time, I will call to your memory the words of the earlier Elizabeth, when, more than three centuries ago, she spoke from her heart, to the Speaker and Members of her last Parliament and said "Though God hath raised me high, yet this I count to the glory of my Crown – that I have reigned with your loves." Now, here in the New World, I say to you that it is my wish that in the years before me I may so reign in Canada and be so remembered.

Queen Elizabeth II
Speech from the Throne
Ottawa, Ontario
October 1957

Governor General Michaëlle Jean signs a Royal Proclamation, dissolving (terminating the life of) the 38th Parliament of Canada and authorizing the holding of a federal election (held on January 23, 2006). Rideau Hall. Ottawa, Ontario. November 29, 2005.

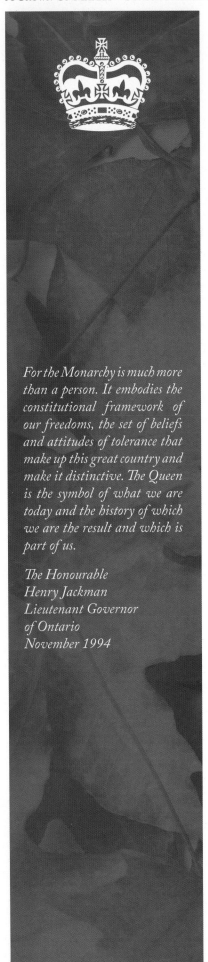

For the Monarchy is much more than a person. It embodies the constitutional framework of our freedoms, the set of beliefs and attitudes of tolerance that make up this great country and make it distinctive. The Queen is the symbol of what we are today and the history of which we are the result and which is part of us.

The Honourable Henry Jackman Lieutenant Governor of Ontario November 1994

Witnessed by Her Excellency the Governor General, Stephen Harper takes his oaths and becomes Canada's 22nd Prime Minister. Rideau Hall. Ottawa, Ontario. February 6, 2006.

Governor General Michaëlle Jean with the newly installed 28th Canadian Ministry under the leadership of Prime Minister Stephen Harper. Rideau Hall. Ottawa, Ontario. February 6, 2006.

Commons or legislature, the Governor General / Lieutenant Governor must follow the advice of the government.

As previously noted, the Governor General or Lieutenant Governor has the reserve power to select a new Prime Minister or Premier if the current one resigns or dies while in office. Although the most common cause for a resignation is the loss of an election, there may be other reasons as well. Normally it is obvious which candidate should be appointed as first minister. However, on occasion the choice might not be clear and the Queen's representative may exercise some discretion with the appointment. Given that the resignation of the Prime Minister or Premier involves the resignation of the entire Cabinet, this reserve power is extremely important. It ensures there will always be a legitimate government in office with the authority to govern.

The representative of the Crown also has the power to dismiss or force the resignation of the Prime Minister or Premier. This is one of the most sensitive decisions that any Governor General or Lieutenant Governor can be called upon to make. It is made only under the most serious circumstances. For example, if a Prime Minister or Premier were to lose the support of a majority in the legislative body on a vote of non-confidence and then refuse to resign, there could be justification for dismissal. In a broader application, a Prime Minister

The uniquely Canadian design of the Queen's Golden Jubilee Flag (2002)

Honouring Our Queen and Our Fellow Citizens
The Coronation (1953), Silver Jubilee (1977) and Golden Jubilee (2002) Medals honour both the Queen and thousands of outstanding Canadians. (12,500, 30,000 and 46,000 respectively were awarded to Canadians).

or the government could be dismissed if the Governor General believes an exceptional situation has created a crisis of confidence in government. This power has been exercised on five occasions in Canadian provinces: Québec in 1878 and 1891 and British Columbia in 1898, 1900 and 1903. This power has not been used in Canada for the federal government, but it was exercised in another Realm of the Commonwealth: by the Governor General of Australia, in 1975.

The Governor General or Lieutenant Governor also has the right to dissolve Parliament or the Legislature. This is normally carried out on advice from the Prime Minister or Premier when an election is sought at the end of a term in office. However, a Prime Minister or Premier can ask for a dissolution at any time. While there are some jurisdictions that have fixed election dates, this does not affect the above-mentioned constitutional principle. Equally, the representative of the Crown can refuse dissolution. In 1926, Governor General Lord Byng exercised reserve power to reject Prime Minister Mackenzie King's advice to dissolve Parliament; instead, the Governor General called upon the Leader of the Opposition to form a government.

As we have seen, the Crown can also, in theory, refuse to give Royal Assent to bills passed by the federal Parliament or provincial legislatures, though this power has been used very seldom.

Although called upon only in extraordinary or extenuating situations, reserve powers of the Crown are in place for a specific purpose. In this regard, they should be seen as a safety valve to be exercised only as a last resort in preserving our democratic system of government.

Canadian rock star Brian Adams unveils a Canada Post stamp honouring the Queen on the occasion of her Golden Jubilee as Queen of Canada. The image is based on a photograph of Her Majesty taken by Adams. Rideau Hall. Ottawa, Ontario. December 2003.

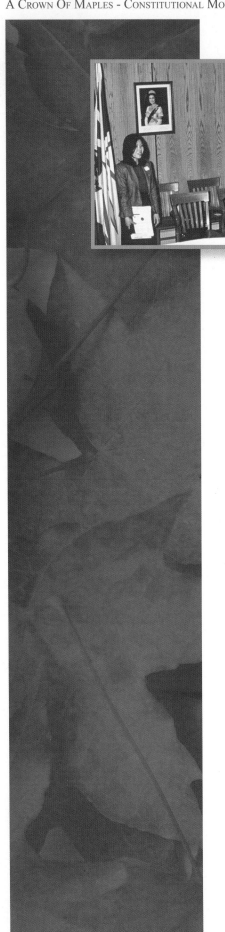

A proud new Canadian citizen poses with her certificate beneath a portrait of the Queen of Canada.

Governor General Michaëlle Jean congratulates a young new Canadian at a special citizenship court on the 60th anniversary of Canadian citizenship. Ottawa, Ontario. February 16, 2007.

The Queen as Head of State: Personifying the Country

As Queen of Canada, Her Majesty Queen Elizabeth II is our head of State and a powerful symbol of Canada and Canadian sovereignty. As citizens of this country, we enjoy the benefit of a hereditary constitutional monarchy that embodies hundreds of years of tradition, mirrors our evolution into full statehood, and represents our democratic principles and institutions.

As the living embodiment of the Crown, Her Majesty is guardian of the Crown's power. At the same time, she unites all Canadians in allegiance and gives a collective sense of belonging to the country. When taking the Oath of Citizenship, new Canadians swear allegiance to the Queen, as do Members of Parliament and the Legislatures, military and police officers. We profess our loyalty to a person who represents all Canadians and not to a document such as a constitution, a banner such as a flag, or a geopolitical entity such as a country. In our constitutional monarchy, these elements are encompassed by the Sovereign.

It is not by accident that, in our daily lives, we hear terms that relate the Crown to the routine operations of government and the country. Whether it is a reference to a royal commission, the Court of Queen's Bench, Crown lands, the Queen's Privy Council for Canada or Crown corporations, all power and honour flow from the Crown. It is a remarkably simple yet powerful principle: Canada is personified by the Sovereign just as the Sovereign is personified by Canada.

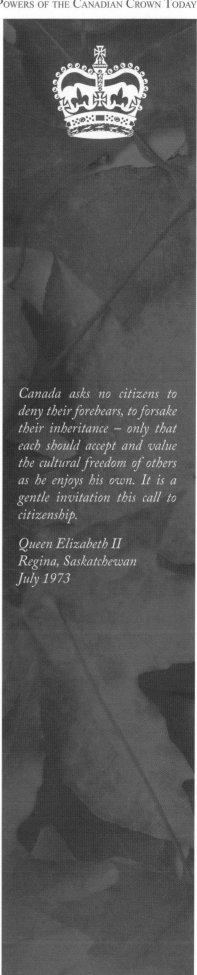

Her Majesty Queen Elizabeth II greets school children from Bjorkdale School who, as part of a science project, travelled to the Canadian Light Source Synchrotron to meet with her. Saskatoon, Saskatchewan. May 2005.

Governor General Jeanne Sauvé and young Canadians mark the Canadian Children's Project "Dear World / Cher Monde". Rideau Hall. Ottawa, Ontario. November 1986.

His Honour Norman Kwong, Lieutenant Governor of Alberta, and Her Honour Mary Kwong stand in front of a portrait of the Queen in the Lieutenant Governor's suite. Edmonton, Alberta.

Canada asks no citizens to deny their forebears, to forsake their inheritance – only that each should accept and value the cultural freedom of others as he enjoys his own. It is a gentle invitation this call to citizenship.

Queen Elizabeth II
Regina, Saskatchewan
July 1973

As the Lieutenant Governor, I have the honour of helping to promote our Canadian traditions. One of my favourite parts of the job is hosting young Albertans at the Legislature. There is a rare, signed 1955 portrait of Her Majesty hanging in the Lieutenant Governor's suite. Every school visit we host at the suite ends with the group posing in front of the portrait to take a picture. Once the group has cleared away, the kids will often sneak back to take a photo of just the Queen. They understand that the portrait is a significant and meaningful symbol. It also tells me that our connection to the Monarchy is a powerful one, that it will endure for generations to come. It will ensure because it is an essential part of who we are as Canadians.

The Honourable Norman Kwong
Lieutenant Governor of Alberta
Edmonton, Alberta
April 2007

Canadian Representatives of the Crown

Chapter 5

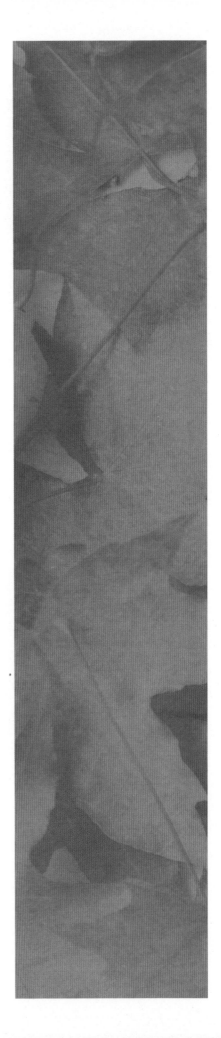

The Governor General's Flag

Government House ("Rideau Hall") is the official residence of Her Majesty The Queen (when in Ottawa) and her representative in the federal jurisdiction – the Governor General.

Canadian Representatives of the Crown

It is understood that the Queen cannot be in Canada at all times. Her principal residence is in London, and she is also Queen of fourteen other Commonwealth countries, sometimes referred to as Realms, in addition to the United Kingdom and Canada. As Queen of Canada, Her Majesty is represented here in federal jurisdiction by the Governor General and in each of our ten provinces by a Lieutenant Governor. Working together with a purpose in common, the 11 vice-regal representatives — with the Governor General as first among equals — exercise powers that flow from the Sovereign. Operating in their own jurisdictions, they personally represent the Queen and perform most of the functions assigned to her as our head of State.

The Governor General

The office of Governor General is the oldest continuous institution in Canada and is an unbroken link with the early days of our country's recorded history. Samuel de Champlain was appointed the first governor of New France in 1627 and was followed by seventeen French governors until 1760. From then until 1867, a total of twenty-one British governors and governors general held office in Canada.

At the time of Confederation, the role of Governor General was very similar to that of a constitutional monarch: advice was given not only by the Canadian Prime Minister, but by his British counterpart as well because, up to 1926, the Governor General represented the Sovereign in Canada as well as the British government. At the Imperial Conference of that year, this somewhat confusing dual arrangement was resolved: the Governor General would represent only the Sovereign. Furthermore, appointments to this office were to be made on the recommendation

Samuel de Champlain (1567 – 1635) - first Governor of New France (1629 – 1635)

Her Excellency the Right Honourable Michaëlle Jean, Governor General of Canada

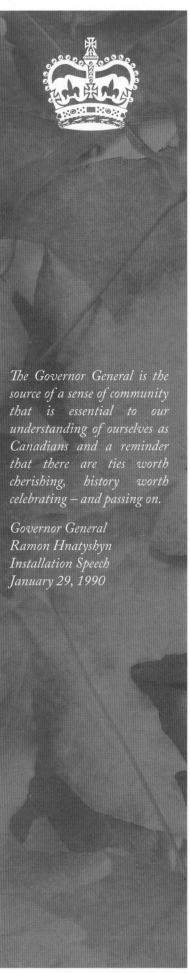

of the Canadian and not the British government. The passage of the *Statute of Westminster, 1931*, which recognized Canada as a self-governing realm, was perhaps the most important development in Canada's evolution as an independent country in the period between Confederation in 1867 and the patriation of our Constitution in 1982. Among other things, it provided that the laws of the United Kingdom Parliament, including those relating to the succession of the Crown, would not apply in Canada or in the Realms without the consent of the Parliament of Canada or the Parliaments of the other Realms. In essence, it outlined the powers that the Canadian parliament (and those of other Realms) held with regard to any changes to the status of its own monarchy — for Canada, it was the Canadian Crown. With this fundamental change, and as Canada continued into full statehood, the office of Governor General also evolved to reflect the new reality that was Canada.

In 1947, Letters Patent of King George VI authorized and empowered the Governor General to exercise most of the royal prerogatives in right of Canada or, in other words, authorities entrusted to George VI in his capacity as King of Canada. In fact, some of these continued to be exercised by the Sovereign on the advice of the Prime Minister. The proclamation of the Canadian Flag in 1965, the appointment of additional senators under special circumstances such as the eight appointments made in 1990, and the creation of honours are prime examples. It rests with Her Majesty to appoint the Governor General, to approve changes to her own title as Queen of Canada, and to fulfill

The Governor General is the source of a sense of community that is essential to our understanding of ourselves as Canadians and a reminder that there are ties worth cherishing, history worth celebrating – and passing on.

Governor General Ramon Hnatyshyn Installation Speech January 29, 1990

The first Governor General to undertake a state visit abroad, Roland Michener serenades a receptive audience during a tour of several Caribbean nations. February - March 1969.

Governor General Jeanne Sauvé greets United States President Ronald Reagan. Rideau Hall. Ottawa, Ontario. April 1987.

Wearing the uniform as Commander-in-Chief of Canada, Governor General Ramon Hnatyshyn presents the Order of Military Merit to Master Corporal Diane Pietraszko. The ceremony is witnessed by the Chief of the Defence Staff, General John de Chastelain. Rideau Hall. Ottawa, Ontario. June 1990.

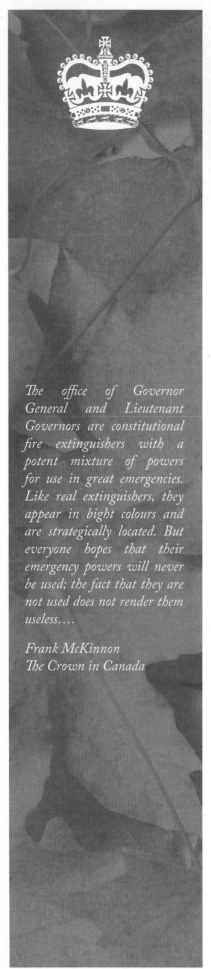

Governor General Roméo LeBlanc greets the delegation from Lesotho having received the letters of credence of the High Commissioner-designate of the Kingdom of Lesotho. May 1995. Governor General Ramon Hnatyshyn poses with the Ambassador of Kuwait, following the presentation of letters of credence ceremony. November 1993.

any other duties that the Prime Minister might advise her to exercise while she is in Canada. The proclamation of the patriation of our Constitution in 1982 was just such an example.

The Governor General's duties cover a broad area of responsibility. First, the Governor General represents the Sovereign in Canada. He or she fulfils most of the duties of Her Majesty including, among others, the granting of Royal Assent, the summoning and dissolution of Parliament, and the use of reserve powers. The Governor General promotes Canadian sovereignty by visiting foreign nations and serving as Commander-in-Chief of Canada for Her Majesty's Canadian Forces. Further, the Governor General accepts Letters of Credence from newly-appointed ambassadors, representatives of non-Commonwealth nations, and those high commissioners, representatives of fellow Commonwealth nations, who do not have the Queen as head of State.

On behalf of Her Majesty, the Governor General recognizes exemplary accomplishments and contributions by awarding honours to Canadians, a subject outlined in detail in a subsequent chapter. Governors General have associated themselves with the pursuit of excellence in many different fields, ranging from physical fitness to the fine arts, from Arctic sovereignty to human rights, and provide an example of leadership to the country through associations with numerous Canadian service, humanitarian and youth groups. For example, the Governor General is the Chief Scout of Canada and the Honorary President of the Canadian Red Cross Society.

Each year, the Governor General presents awards to deserving Canadians in a wide range of fields. Accomplishment and excellence are publicly acknowledged in areas such as literacy, journalism, visual and media arts, architecture and the performing arts. In addition, distinguished Canadians are celebrated with the Governor General's Caring Canadian Award, the Governor General's Academic Medal, the Governor General's Northern Medal, the Governor General's Award in Commemoration of the Persons Case, the Governor General's Award for Excellence in Teaching Canadian History, among others. In every case, the Canadian Crown acknowledges the respect and gratitude of all citizens for these outstanding Canadians who contribute to our country as well as to our collective sense of pride and identity.

Perhaps the principal role of the Governor General, beyond constitutional duties, is to promote national identity and unity. Through extensive visits to all regions of the country, involvement in many cultural and awards ceremonies, and the delivery of major addresses, the Governor General makes all Canadians aware of the rich and colourful tapestry of our national identity. It is through an appreciation of ourselves as a unique people that all of us come to a fuller appreciation of our unity and pride in country.

In 1952, the appointment of Vincent Massey ushered in a new era in both the history of the office of Governor General and of Canada. Governors General would now be Canadian citizens who represented Her Majesty The Queen and, at the same time, were a true and accurate reflection of the richness of Canadian society. Over more than half a century, the ten Governors General — Vincent Massey, Georges P. Vanier, Roland Michener, Jules Léger, Edward Schreyer, Jeanne Sauvé, Ramon Hnatyshyn, Roméo LeBlanc, Adrienne Clarkson and Michaëlle Jean — have been drawn from all regions of the country, mirrored our bilingual and multicultural reality and, above all else, demonstrated a strong desire to represent the Canadian Crown with dignity and to use the office to highlight the best that is Canada and in being Canadian.

The Governor General, who bears the title "Excellency" during office along with his/her spouse, is appointed by the Queen on the recommendation of the Prime Minister and normally holds office for five years. The Governor General bears the title "Right Honourable" for life.

The Lieutenant Governors

Each of the ten Canadian provinces has a Lieutenant Governor. He or she is the personal representative of the Queen and is appointed by the Prime Minister. The three territories — Northwest Territories, Yukon and Nunavut, which receive authority from the Parliament of Canada, exercise many of the powers similar to those of the provinces. However, unlike the provinces, they do not have a direct representative of the Sovereign. Instead, they have a Commissioner who performs some similar functions.

In the early years after Confederation, Lieutenant Governors were seen as the representatives of the Governor General and agents of

The Honourable Pauline M. McGibbon, Lieutenant Governor of Ontario (1974 – 1980) – the first female representative of the Queen in Canada.

The Honourable Ralph G. Steinhauer, Lieutenant Governor of Alberta (1974 – 1979) – the first Aboriginal representative of the Queen in Canada.

Colonel the Honourable Lincoln M. Alexander, Lieutenant Governor of Ontario (1985 – 1991) – the first Black representative of the Queen in Canada.

His Honour Herménégilde Chiasson, Lieutenant Governor of New Brunswick, signs the roll at the swearing-in ceremony for Members of the Legislative Assembly. Fredericton, New Brunswick. October 2006.

Her Honour Mayann Francis, Lieutenant Governor of Nova Scotia, greets major supports / senior volunteers of the United Way of Halifax Region at a reception in their honour. Halifax, Nova Scotia. February 2007.

the federal government, rather than as direct representatives of the Sovereign. Dating back to 1872, legal judgements relating to the office and the evolution of Canadian federalism have further clarified and confirmed the status of Lieutenant Governor as direct representative of the Crown in the provinces. Although they continue to be appointed and paid by the federal government, they are the representatives of the Queen and, thereby, the embodiment of the Crown in the provinces.

Lieutenant Governors fulfil the responsibilities and functions of the Sovereign in the provinces as does the Governor General in federal jurisdiction. In their respective jurisdictions, they exercise the powers of the Queen as head of State and symbolize provincial sovereignty and constitutional status as full members within Canadian Confederation. As well, Lieutenant Governors lend the prestige of their offices and devote a great deal of time to the promotion of worthy causes as they travel extensively throughout their provinces.

Over the past three decades, the appointment of Lieutenant Governors has increasingly reflected a more accurate image of the modern face of Canadian society. Drawn from the Aboriginal and artistic communities, visibility minority groups, the disability community, the private and public sectors to name but a few, Lieutenant Governors are also a very public mirror of the richness and diversity of the Canadian Crown. As is the case with the Governor General, an important function of the Lieutenant Governors is to present honours and awards to deserving citizens who have made a difference in the life of their province and, by extension, their country. By its very presence, this public and visible role of the Canadian Crown and its representatives lends dignity and honour that warrants the gratitude of all citizens.

Lieutenant Governors are appointed for a term of office of not less than five years and bear the title "His/Her Honour" during office, as do their spouses. Lieutenant Governors bear the title "Honourable" for life.

The Canadian Essence of Monarchy

As a sovereign parliamentary democracy, Canada benefits from the prestige, history and honour that flow from a hereditary monarchy spanning hundreds of years. Some may think it a contradiction to have such an ancient and historic institution forming part of a modern political state. However, beyond the vital constitutional duties performed by the Crown, the reality is that monarchy has continued to evolve, has been adopted voluntarily by Canada and transformed into a contemporary and relevant Canadian institution.

As previously mentioned, the Letters Patent of 1947 defined the authority of the Governor General and expressly authorized and empowered the Governor General to exercise most prerogatives, powers and authorities that His Majesty held as King of Canada. Such action has served to reinforce the workings of the Crown in the daily life of Canada. Since that time, the Crown in Right of Canada has proclaimed a national flag, created a system of Canadian honours, and patriated our Constitution, which includes the *Canadian Charter of Rights and Freedom*. As well, other prerogative powers of the Sovereign, such as the issuing of Letters of Credence to ambassadors and the granting of armorial bearings (coats of arms) to Canadians, have been transferred for exercise in Canada.

While Canada has quite correctly made the institution of the Crown its very own over the course of several decades, its Canadian representatives — the Governor General and Lieutenant Governors — continue to derive their powers from the Sovereign and act on her behalf as Queen of Canada.

The Crown is truly Canadian through the Queen and her eleven Canadian representatives. Individuals appointed to the offices of Governor General and Lieutenant Governor have exemplified the finest example of Canadian citizenship and the values we all share. Since the appointment in 1952 of the Right Honourable Vincent Massey — the first Governor General to be born in Canada since Pierre de Vaudreuil in 1755 — all representatives of the Queen in this country have been Canadian citizens who have distinguished themselves in service to the country.

The Queen and her family take a very personal and sustained interest in Canada, its people, and the concerns that all Canadians share.

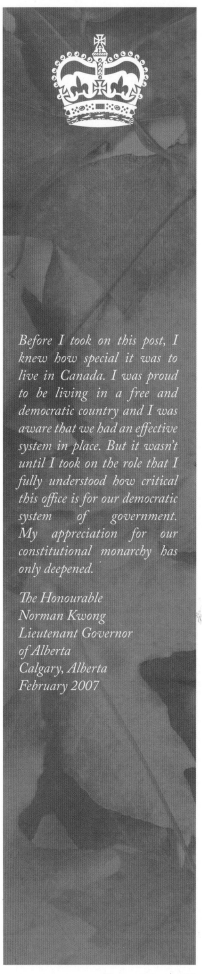

Before I took on this post, I knew how special it was to live in Canada. I was proud to be living in a free and democratic country and I was aware that we had an effective system in place. But it wasn't until I took on the role that I fully understood how critical this office is for our democratic system of government. My appreciation for our constitutional monarchy has only deepened.

*The Honourable
Norman Kwong
Lieutenant Governor
of Alberta
Calgary, Alberta
February 2007*

Regardless of the era, anxious young Canadians eagerly await the arrival of their Sovereign (1939 and 1987).

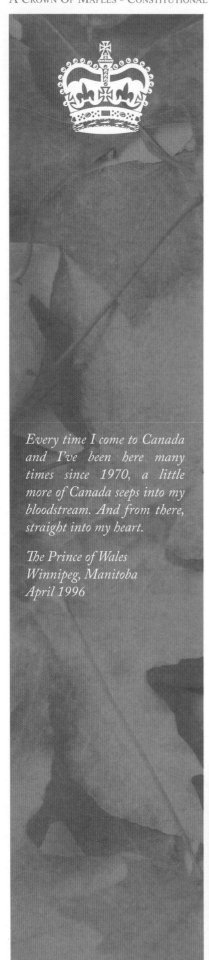

Every time I come to Canada and I've been here many times since 1970, a little more of Canada seeps into my bloodstream. And from there, straight into my heart.

*The Prince of Wales
Winnipeg, Manitoba
April 1996*

Issues such as the environment, medical research, arts and culture, literacy, voluntary action and national unity have been singled out for attention by the Crown and its representatives in all regions of the country. The frequency of royal visits to Canada serves not only to remind Canadians of the relevance of this institution, but also to raise awareness of the various issues and concerns that have an impact on our society every day.

We have seen that the role of the Crown and its representatives — the Sovereign, the Governor General and Lieutenant Governors — has continued to evolve just as our country itself has matured to full statehood. Canada has adapted the Crown to suit its own needs and purposes to the point where it clearly reflects our regional, bilingual and multicultural character.

In every sense of the word, it is the Canadian Crown.

His Royal Highness The Prince of Wales, with Princes William and Harry, sporting their true Canadian colours at Canada Place (Pacific Marine Heritage Legacy). Vancouver, British Columbia. March 1998.

The Prince of Wales "does a jig" in celebrating a gift (a Royal Canadian Air Force Tartan kilt) presented to him by the Commanding Officer of Canadian Forces Base Moose Jaw (NATO Flight Training Centre) . Moose Jaw, Saskatchewan. April 2001.

The Prince of Wales speaks with young Canadians at the SS Klondike National Historic Site. Whitehorse, Yukon. April 2001.

The cap badge of the Royal 22ⁿᵈ Regiment ("The Van Doos")

A distinguished and highly decorated soldier, Governor General Georges Vanier held the rank of Major-General. He was a founding member of the famous Royal 22ⁿᵈ Regiment, which he went on to command and serve as "Colonel of the Regiment".

The Badge of Her Majesty's Canadian Forces (HMCF)

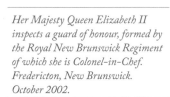

Her Majesty Queen Elizabeth II enjoys a chat with Canadian veterans on the grounds of the Alberta Legislature. Edmonton, Alberta. May 2005.

Her Majesty Queen Elizabeth II inspects a guard of honour, formed by the Royal New Brunswick Regiment of which she is Colonel-in-Chief. Fredericton, New Brunswick. October 2002.

As their Colonel-in-Chief, Her Majesty Queen Elizabeth II presents new Colours to the Argyll and Sutherland Highlanders of Canada (Princess Louise's). Hamilton, Ontario. October 2002.

I have been pleased to grant you the distinction of carrying my cipher emblazoned on the Regimental Colour. In doing so, I hope you will continue to build on the traditions of the past and strive to reflect them in service to your country as both citizens and soldiers. Canada Gu-Brath. (Canada Forever)

Queen Elizabeth II
Presentation of Colours Ceremony
Hamilton, Ontario
October 2002

Comparison With Other Systems of Government

Chapter 6

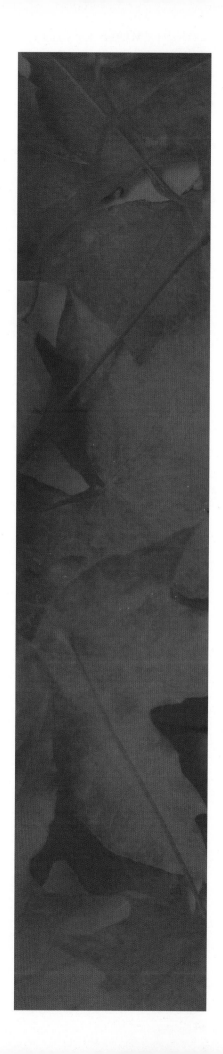

The maple leaf flag flies over the Canadian Embassy in Washington, D.C., with the U.S. Capital Building in the background.

O ur form of government shares many similarities with those of some nations while having many differences with others.

An interesting comparison can be made between our system of parliamentary democracy and that of our closest neighbour, the United States of America. Unlike Canada, the United States is a republic with a congressional democracy and a presidential system of government. The president serves as both head of State and head of Government, a distinction made in Canada between the Queen and the Prime Minister. In the United States, no distinction is made between the person who formally holds power and the person who uses it. As head of Government, the president is a political figure who, as head of State, is also expected to serve as a non-partisan symbol of all citizens of the country.

In a congressional democracy such as the United States, there is a clear separation of powers between the executive — the President and cabinet, and the legislative — Congress, branches of government. Indeed, the President and cabinet cannot be members of Congress and are not directly accountable to the elected representatives of the people as they are in Canada. Question Period in the federal Parliament or provincial legislatures demonstrates that, in a parliamentary democracy, accountability is an important daily feature of our system. The Prime Minister, as a member of Parliament and leader of the party commanding the confidence of the House of Commons, and cabinet ministers must appear in Parliament to answer questions, explain actions, and defend policies before the representatives of the people. So too must the provincial Premiers and ministers in their legislatures.

The National Flag of Canada and the United States of America

The Queen's Personal Canadian Flag flies from the Peace Tower when Her Majesty is on Parliament Hill.

The almost two hundred nations in the world have numerous different forms and systems of government. Many are republics — nations with an elected or nominated president — with variations of a congressional and/or parliamentary democracy. Still others are similar to Canada in that they are constitutional monarchies. Of the fifty-three members of the Commonwealth of Nations, sixteen[1] recognize the Queen as their head of State. Each one is a constitutional monarchy in its own right. All these Realms, other than the United Kingdom (where the Queen resides), have a Governor General representing the Sovereign. Of these sixteen nations, two have more than one representative of the Queen: Canada has eleven, a Governor General and ten Lieutenant Governors in the provinces, and Australia has seven, a Governor General and six Governors in the states.

Of the remaining thirty-seven Commonwealth members, most are republics while a few have their own monarchies. At the same time, all fifty-three nations recognize Queen Elizabeth II as "Head of the Commonwealth." In this way, the Queen is the visible embodiment of this free association of nations that spans all continents and forms a bridge of understanding and cooperation between almost thirty per cent of the world's population — some two billion people.

In the one system [a monarchy] the soul of the nation is emphasized, in the other [a republic] merely the fact of a government....

Frank MacKinnon
The Crown in Canada

---

1 Antigua and Barbuda, Australia, Bahamas. Barbados, Belize, Canada, Grenada, Jamaica, New Zealand, Papua New Guinea, Saint Christopher and Nevis, Saint Lucia, Saint Vincent and the Grenadines, Solomon Islands, Tuvalu, the United Kingdom.

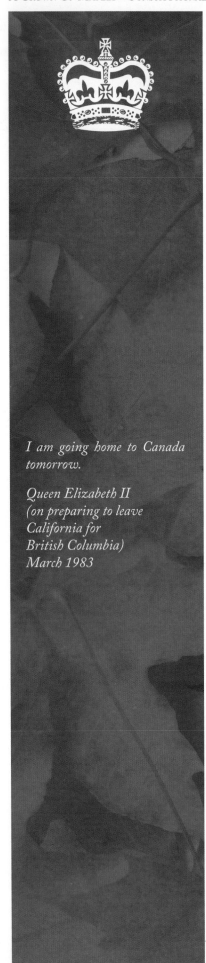

I am going home to Canada tomorrow.

Queen Elizabeth II (on preparing to leave California for British Columbia) March 1983

Constitutional monarchy is not limited to the Commonwealth. Indeed, there are nineteen[2] other constitutional monarchies outside the Commonwealth. While some are fairly young in terms of history, others have existed for hundreds of years.

Perhaps the most remarkable characteristic of constitutional monarchy is how well it works in a wide variety of countries around the world. Although based on time-honoured principles and powers, monarchy has been consistently and effectively adapted to meet the contemporary needs of nations and their citizens. In these the early years of the twenty-first century, constitutional monarchy remains a well-suited and relevant political institution.

Queen Elizabeth II, escorted by Commonwealth Secretary-General Don McKinnon, greets Archbishop Tutu at a Commonwealth celebration at Westminster Abbey on Commonwealth Day 2004 (a Canadian flag and youth from across the Commonwealth form the backdrop).

2 Andorra, Bahrain, Belgium, Cambodia, Denmark, Japan, Jordan, Kuwait, Liechtenstein, Luxembourg, Monaco, Morocco, Nepal, Norway, Spain, Sweden, Thailand, The Netherlands, United Arab Emirates

Her Majesty Queen Elizabeth II congratulates singer/actress Ginette Reno, opera star Measha Brueggergosman and legendary jazz pianist/composer Oscar Peterson following a Golden Jubilee Gala Concert at Roy Thomson Hall. Toronto, Ontario. October 2002.

Her Majesty Queen Elizabeth II enjoys a dance performance by the Riel Reelers at a provincial luncheon held in the Lumsden Sports Centre. Lumsden, Saskatchewan. May 2005.

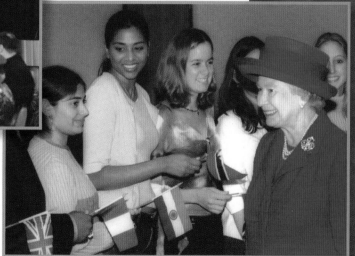

Her Majesty Queen Elizabeth II greets students from across the Commonwealth during a visit to Sheridan College. Oakville, Ontario. October 2002.

It [the Crown] is part of ourselves. It is linked in a very special way with our national life. It stands for qualities and institutions which mean Canada to every one of us and which for all our differences and all our variety have kept Canada Canadian. How much the Crown has done to give us our individual character as a nation in the Americas!

Governor General Vincent Massey
Radio Broadcast, 1953

The Visual Presence of the Canadian Crown

Chapter 7

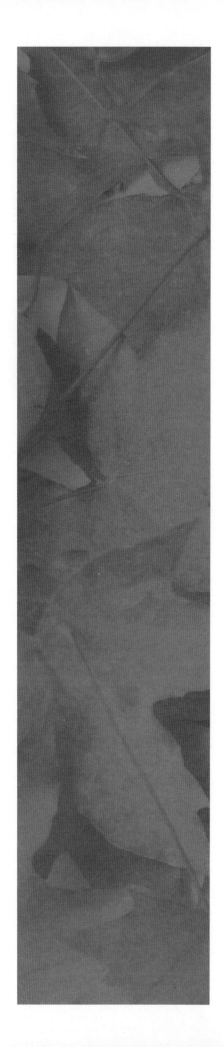

The Canada Post stamp celebrating Her Majesty The Queen's 80th birthday (2006)

Happy Birthday! April 21, 1926 / Joyeux anniversaire! 21 avril 1926

Canada 51

Queen Elizabeth II visits the RCMP Musical Ride Equitation Centre. Ottawa, Ontario. October 2002.

The Crown as A Symbol of Statehood

Every country has symbols — flags, coats of arms, events, and historical figures, among others — that foster among its citizens a sense of pride in being part of the larger "national family." Canada is a land of diversity, embracing vast differences within its borders and among its people. Symbols have provided connections across great expanses of space and time and have been a source of both pride and unity. In this regard, perhaps our most visible symbol is the Canadian Crown.

It is possible to find symbols of the Crown displayed in many important areas: coinage and currency, constitutional documents, postage stamps, police and military insignia, government coats of arms and court buildings, to name but a few. In addition, there are approximately seventy prominent Canadian organizations with royal designation, such as the Royal Canadian Legion and the Royal Winnipeg Ballet, which were granted this honour personally by the Sovereign. Approximately forty military regiments have the Queen or a member of the Royal Family as colonel-in-chief; many carry "Royal" designation, such as the Royal 22e Régiment and the Royal New Brunswick Regiment, as well as other forces such as the Royal Canadian Mounted Police and the Royal Newfoundland Constabulary. Indeed, all naval vessels of Her Majesty's Canadian Forces are named with the prefix H.M.C.S. — Her Majesty's Canadian

The Queen Elizabeth Way (one of Ontario's busiest highways) was named for the mother of Queen Elizabeth II. Bearing the Crown, these signs are somewhat similar to Ontario's usual "King's Highway" signs.

QEW — ONTARIO

Queen Elizabeth II's effigy on the Canadian dollar coin and portrait on the twenty dollar bill

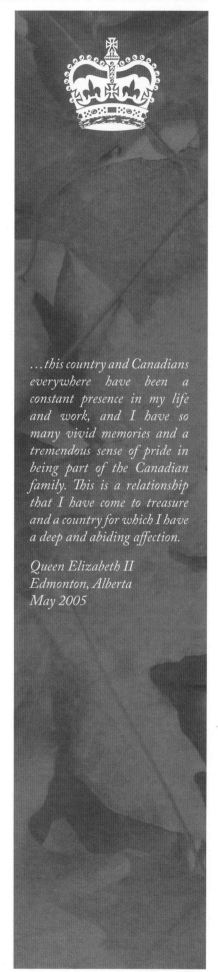

Ship. These and many other examples are enduring and appropriate reminders that power and honour flow from the Crown of Canada.

As our head of State, the Queen and her representatives serve to embody who we are as a people and a country by representing the values, goals and aspirations that we all share.

Further, the collective Crown — the Sovereign, the Governor General and the Lieutenant Governors — also serves as a symbol to other nations that Canada is a sovereign country. Beyond explaining our system of government, the representatives of the Crown use history, tradition and pageantry in giving daily expression to our national identity on behalf of all Canadians.

Canadian Honours of the Crown

In a constitutional monarchy, the Sovereign is the source or "fount" of all honours. This means that honours and decorations are created by and conferred in the name of the Queen, and on behalf of all Canadians, in the recognition of meritorious service or accomplishment. Indeed, honours are the highest form of recognition given to a person and are dynamic symbols of Canadian identity, unity and pride.

As part of Government House in Ottawa — the Office of the Governor General, the Chancellery of Honours administers all aspects of Canada's Honours System, including national honours and heraldry. Canada's highest honour is the Order of Canada that is awarded in three levels — Companion, Officer and Member. This pattern is also found in the other national orders: the Order of Military Merit

...this country and Canadians everywhere have been a constant presence in my life and work, and I have so many vivid memories and a tremendous sense of pride in being part of the Canadian family. This is a relationship that I have come to treasure and a country for which I have a deep and abiding affection.

Queen Elizabeth II
Edmonton, Alberta
May 2005

Badges proudly surmounted by the St. Edward's Crown:
1 *The Royal Canadian Mounted Police*
2 *The Ontario Provincial Police*
3 *The Royal Newfoundland Constabulary*
4 *The Canadian Security Intelligence Service*
5 *The Cape Breton Regional Police Service*
6 *The Royal Canadian Legion*
7 *The Vancouver Police Department*

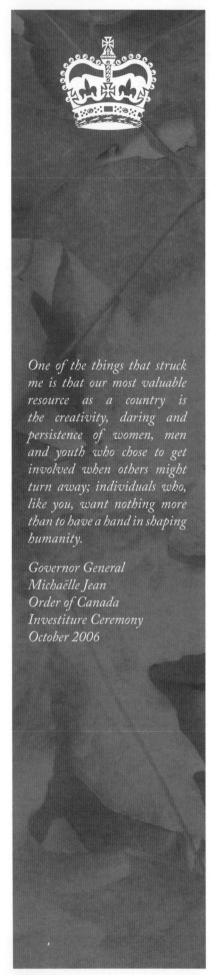

The insignia of a Companion of the Order of Canada. Her Majesty The Queen is Sovereign of the Order. Companions, Officers and Members inducted into the Order by the Governor General are done so in the name of the Queen.

Queen Elizabeth II invests Jules Léger (later Governor General of Canada 1974 – 1979) as a Companion of the Order of Canada. Rideau Hall. Ottawa, Ontario. August 1973.

The first living person to be made an honorary Canadian citizen, Nelson Mandela is congratulated by Governor General Roméo LeBlanc on being made an honorary Companion of the Order of Canada. Rideau Hall. Ottawa, Ontario. September 1998.

(Commander, Officer and Member), the Order of Merit of the Police Forces (Companion, Officer and Member), the Royal Victorian Order (Commander, Lieutenant and Members — conferred personally by Her Majesty The Queen), and the Most Venerable Order of the Hospital of St. John of Jerusalem (Knight/Dame, Commander, Officer and Member).

Decorations recognizing degrees of bravery, professionalism and exceptional devotion to duty include: Military Valour Decorations (Victoria Cross, Star of Military Valour and Medal of Military Valour), Decorations for Bravery (Cross of Valour, Star of Courage and Medal of Bravery) and Meritorious Service Decorations (Meritorious Service Cross and Meritorious Service Medal-Military and Civil Divisions).

The Governor General conducts investiture ceremonies in the name of the Queen. The honours conferred bear the Crown as a visible reminder of a key point: all such honours are granted by the Sovereign on behalf of the entire country.

All ten provinces have established orders. Examples, bearing the St. Edward's Crown, are: the Order of Newfoundland and Labrador, the Order of Ontario and the Order of British Columbia.

Governor General Adrienne Clarkson presents a National Native Role Model Award to Marie Smith-Tutin. Rideau Hall. Ottawa, Ontario. April 2000.

For her bravery during a skyjacking in 1971, flight attendant Mary Dohey became the first woman to be awarded the Cross of Valour by Governor General Jules Léger. Rideau Hall. Ottawa, Ontario. February 1976.

Legendary writer, composer and recording artist Leonard Cohen is congratulated by Governor General Ramon Hnatyshyn upon being presented with the Governor General's Award for Lifetime Artistic Achievement. Rideau Hall. Ottawa, Ontario. November 1993.

Although all provinces and territories have a series of awards, the ten provinces in particular have established orders: L'Ordre national du Québec; The Saskatchewan Order of Merit; The Order of Ontario; The Order of British Columbia; The Alberta Order of Excellence; The Order of Prince Edward Island; The Order of Manitoba; The Order of New Brunswick; The Order of Nova Scotia; and The Order of Newfoundland and Labrador.

Another form of honour flowing from the Crown is the granting of armorial bearings or coats of arms. Part of the Chancellery, the Canadian Heraldic Authority was established in 1988 flowing from Royal Letters Patent and provides a Canadian mechanism for the granting of heraldic emblems to Canadian governments, communities, corporations, associations and individuals. Recognizing the importance of heraldic symbols in fostering national identity and pride, the Authority grants uniquely Canadian emblems in the name of the Queen of Canada and uses this ancient and colourful science to highlight our collective heritage and identity.

The Arms of the Canadian Heraldic Authority

The Badge of the Siksika Nation

His Royal Highness The Prince Edward (now The Earl of Wessex) presents Royal Letters Patent to Governor General Jeanne Sauvé. Rideau Hall. Ottawa, Ontario. June 1988. (With this document, coats-of-arms would be granted to Canadians in Canada by the Canadian Crown.)

Presentation of badge to the Siksika Nation by Governor General Ramon Hnatyshyn. This was the first grant of a heraldic emblem to a First Nations government in Canada. Gleichen, Alberta. October 1990.

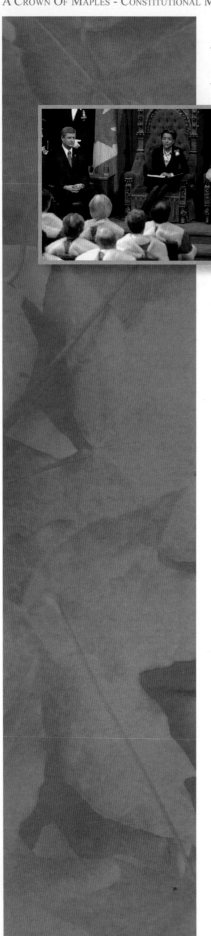

Governor General Michaëlle Jean reads the Speech from the Throne in the Senate Chamber. October 2007.

Ceremonial Occasions

The Queen and her representatives devote much time and energy to ceremonial duties. Such duties are an important part of the life of our country: the royal pageantry, ceremony and traditions of the Queen, the Governor General and the Lieutenant Governors all enhance our sense of identity and reflect our rich and vibrant traditions.

Most often, the Governor General or Lieutenant Governors perform ceremonial functions on behalf of the Queen in her absence. All such functions have dynamic and symbolic elements that identify the presence of the Crown. The Queen and her representatives in Canada each have their own personal flags, which are flown in their presence. As well, guards of honour, gun salutes and the playing of Canada's Royal Anthem "God Save The Queen" and National Anthem "O Canada" are all reminders that such official honours are reserved for Canada's head of State, whose presence helps to unify the entire country by making us all more aware of the national community we share.

Victoria Day, observed on the first Monday preceding May 25, was established as a national holiday in 1901 by the Canadian Parliament. "The Queen's Birthday" celebrates the birthdays of Queen Victoria (May 24, 1819) and Queen Elizabeth, whose actual birthday is April 21, 1926.

Governor General Roland Michener presents the Order of Canada to Lester Pearson. The Order was instituted on April 17, 1967 by Queen Elizabeth II on the advice of Prime Minister Pearson. Rideau Hall. Ottawa, Ontario. November 1968.

Governor General Ed Schreyer is presented with the parliamentary address (leading to the eventual patriation of the Constitution) by the Speaker of the House of Commons, Jeanne Sauvé. Two and a half years later, Mme Sauvé succeeded Mr. Schreyer as Canada's 23ʳᵈ Governor General. Rideau Hall, Ottawa, Ontario. December 1981.

Royal Visits

Today, Canadians are quite familiar with visits by the Queen and members of her family. Modern means of transportation and communication have made such visits an almost annual part of our national life and serve to bring the Crown into very personal contact with the people it represents — all Canadians, regardless of language, race, colour or religion.

King George VI and Queen Elizabeth (parents of Queen Elizabeth II) during the historic 1939 Royal Visit to Canada.

Queen Elizabeth II and The Duke of Edinburgh at Edmonton City Hall. Edmonton, Alberta. May 2005.

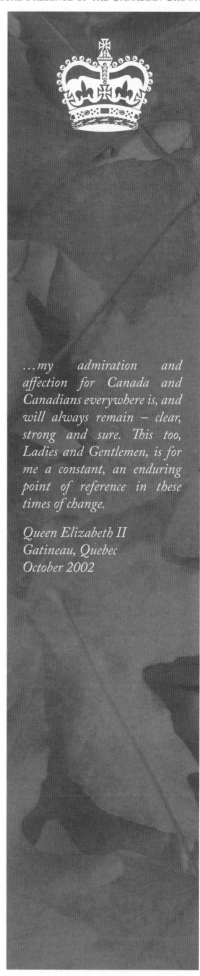

...my admiration and affection for Canada and Canadians everywhere is, and will always remain – clear, strong and sure. This too, Ladies and Gentlemen, is for me a constant, an enduring point of reference in these times of change.

Queen Elizabeth II
Gatineau, Quebec
October 2002

Although members of the Sovereign's family have been visiting Canada for well over two hundred years, it was only in 1939 that a reigning monarch arrived on our shores. In that year, King George VI and Queen Elizabeth, later Queen Elizabeth the Queen Mother, undertook an extensive six-week tour across Canada and endeared themselves to every single Canadian they met. The first visit by Queen Elizabeth II was made in 1951 when, as Princess Elizabeth, she and her husband, the Duke of Edinburgh, began their close and enduring association with Canada.

Through a deliberate effort to visit every province and territory, the Queen and members of her family have developed an extensive knowledge of and affection for all parts of this land and its people. In much the same way, royal visits put a very human face on royalty and allow Canadians to express the affection and admiration that is so genuine and evident during such visits.

In addition to providing a focus for the strong bond between Canadians and their Sovereign, royal visits are a very real reminder of our collective heritage and status as both a constitutional monarchy and a parliamentary democracy. The Queen and members of her family frequently use such visits to associate themselves with worthy causes. For example, the Duke of Edinburgh and the Earl of Wessex (Prince Edward) are strong supporters of the Duke of Edinburgh's Awards, which encourage young people to excel to the best of their abilities and talents. The Princess Royal (Princess Anne) is President of the Save the Children Fund and fosters a greater understanding among all people about the

A Canadian holds an earlier portrait of Her Majesty The Queen during the walkabout at Old Government House in Fredericton, New Brunswick. October 2002.

The connection between Her Majesty and Canadians is enduring and deeply rooted. Her genuine affection for our country and our people extends beyond her role as Sovereign. Canadians recognize this heartfelt kinship and have reciprocated with great fondness and admiration….

*Governor General
Michaëlle Jean
Victoria Day Message
May 2007*

plight of disadvantaged children. Royal visits have, therefore, a unique way of contributing to our understanding of who we are as members of the Canadian family and our place within the community of nations.

While in Canada, the Queen and members of her family often lend support to other noteworthy causes that mirror the ongoing themes of office chosen by the Governor General and/or Lieutenant Governors. The need for environmental preservation, the plight of socially disadvantaged people, the role of voluntarism and community service, the promise of scientific and medical research, and the creation of new educational skill sets are but a few of these subjects that warrant enhanced public attention and action. With the exposure gained through royal visits, timely issues are kept in the public consciousness and highlighted as a part of a sustained commitment to the building of a stronger and more inclusive society.

Increasingly, themes are developed that serve to provide a comprehensive framework for all royal visit programming. For example, Her Majesty The Queen and His Royal Highness The Duke of Edinburgh visited Saskatchewan and Alberta in 2005 to pay tribute to the 100th anniversary of the entry of these two provinces into Confederation. Quite appropriately, the theme was "Honouring the Spirit of Nation Builders," combining a tribute to past and present community builders while challenging youth to envisage and shape the Canada of the future. As with all such visits, the intent is to bring to life the institution of the Canadian Crown through close-up encounters and the active involvement of as many Canadians as possible.

Official royal visits to Canada are coordinated by the Department of Canadian Heritage in association with the provinces and/or territories included in the itinerary.

The Canada Post definitive stamp of Her Majesty The Queen.

Queen Elizabeth II visits the Canadian Light Source Synchrotron. Saskatoon, Saskatchewan. May 2005.

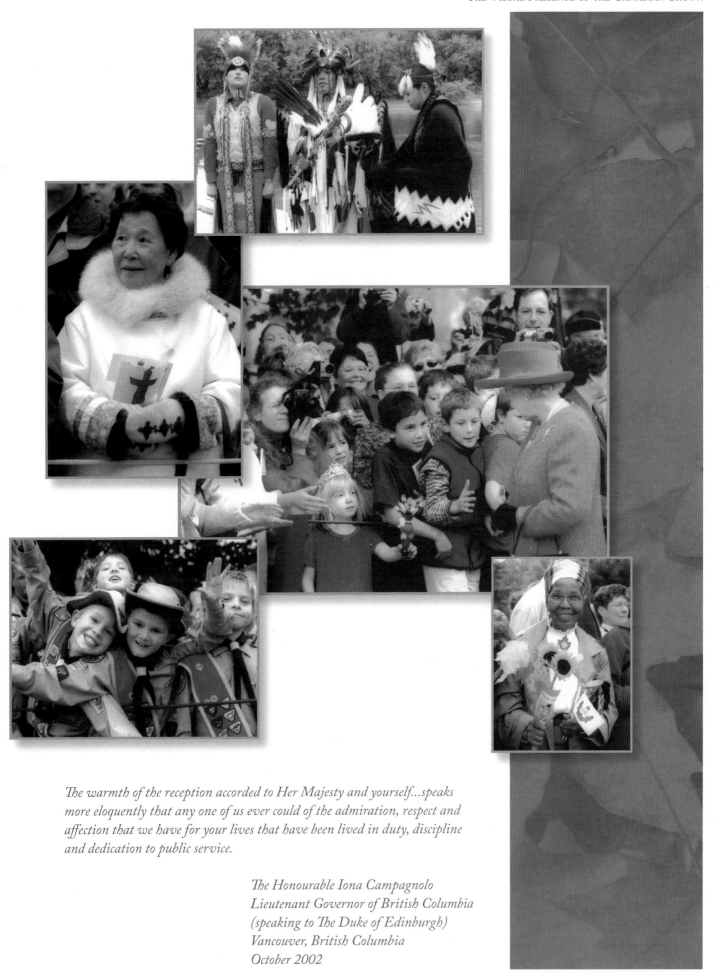

The warmth of the reception accorded to Her Majesty and yourself...speaks more eloquently that any one of us ever could of the admiration, respect and affection that we have for your lives that have been lived in duty, discipline and dedication to public service.

The Honourable Iona Campagnolo
Lieutenant Governor of British Columbia
(speaking to The Duke of Edinburgh)
Vancouver, British Columbia
October 2002

Conclusion

Chapter 8

Conclusion

As a bilingual, multicultural society in a parliamentary democracy, Canada has steadily evolved as a sovereign and confident country. Our history is as varied as it is colourful and Canadians have successfully laid the foundations for a dynamic cultural fabric within the framework of stable, democratic institutions. In this context, the Crown of Canada must be seen not only as an enduring part of our living history, but also as a fundamental and relevant political institution.

As Canada has changed, and continues to adapt to address new challenges and circumstances, so too has the Crown. In both the federal and provincial jurisdictions, the Crown and its representatives reflect the reality of contemporary Canada. The Fathers of Confederation had great foresight in their retention of constitutional monarchy — not merely as a historical institution, but as one that provided the benefits of continuity and stability.

Throughout our history, the Crown has been present to ensure continuity and the preservation of our democratic principles by encouraging a common dedication to the precepts of justice and equality. It would be a serious error to misinterpret its "behind the scenes" low-key approach as reflecting a degree of irrelevance. On the contrary, the Crown remains an important democratic institution in Canada and serves as the vigilant guardian of our system of government during times of constant change. Beyond the obvious pageantry, it functions as a safeguard for rights and freedoms that is used under special circumstances that can arise in even the most democratic of countries.

Queen Elizabeth II enjoys a light moment with crew of the Royal Flight (Canadian Forces Airbus) upon arrival at 12 Wing (Sidney) to begin her Golden Jubilee visit to British Columbia. Sidney, British Columbia. October 2002.

The Royal Cypher is the personal device or monogram of Her Majesty The Queen (EIIR refers to Elizabeth II and R is for Regina, meaning Queen) surmounted by the St. Edward's Crown. A symbol of sovereignty, the cypher is used in the insignia of Canadian orders, decorations and medals and on various badges. (In this instance, the cypher is shown centred among a garland of maple leaves).

Constitutional monarchy remains a valuable asset to democracy in many nations. Although based on time-honoured traditions and customs, it has proven remarkably well-suited to a modern world that faces constant pressures on its democratic institutions.

Apart from its important functions in the operation of our system of government, the collective Crown — the Sovereign, the Governor General and Lieutenant Governors — means much to Canadians. It represents our democratic traditions as well as our collective sense of heritage and identity. Heritage and tradition remain vital even in our fast-paced, technologically-advanced society. No wise nation would

Queen Elizabeth II receives flowers from a patient at Maison Michel-Sarazin. Sillery, Quebec. October 1987.

Queen Elizabeth II speaks with Inuit residents. Rankin Inlet, Northwest Territories (now Nunavut). August 1994.

Queen Elizabeth II officiates at the "dropping of the puck" ceremony for a Vancouver Canucks – San Jose Sharks hockey game at GM Place. Vancouver, British Columbia. October 2002.

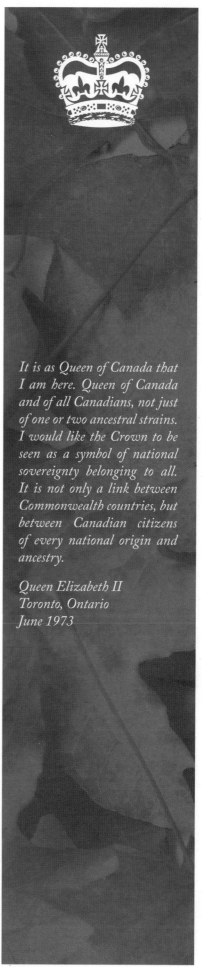

It is as Queen of Canada that I am here. Queen of Canada and of all Canadians, not just of one or two ancestral strains. I would like the Crown to be seen as a symbol of national sovereignty belonging to all. It is not only a link between Commonwealth countries, but between Canadian citizens of every national origin and ancestry.

Queen Elizabeth II
Toronto, Ontario
June 1973

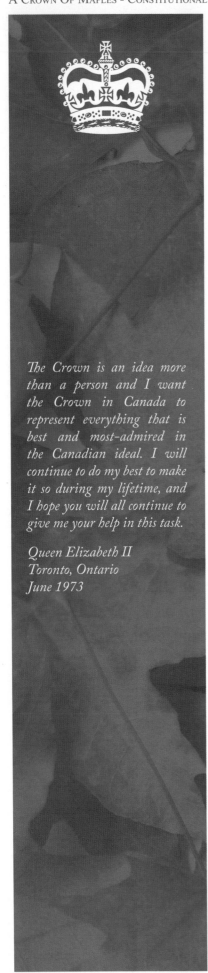

The Crown is an idea more than a person and I want the Crown in Canada to represent everything that is best and most-admired in the Canadian ideal. I will continue to do my best to make it so during my lifetime, and I hope you will all continue to give me your help in this task.

Queen Elizabeth II
Toronto, Ontario
June 1973

deny their importance for they provide us with a sense of our past and a guide for our future in a complex, challenging world.

The Crown of Canada is not merely a symbol or tradition. In every respect, it represents the humanity of our country and speaks eloquently of the collective spirit that makes us truly Canadian.

Governor General Ed Schreyer in conversation with Canadian hero Terry Fox during his Marathon of Hope run across Canada. Rideau Hall. Ottawa, Ontario. June 1980.

Governor General Michaëlle Jean admires a portrait of Her Majesty The Queen affixed to the ceiling of the submarine HMCS Windsor. Halifax, Nova Scotia. May 2006.

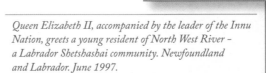

Queen Elizabeth II, accompanied by the leader of the Innu Nation, greets a young resident of North West River - a Labrador Shetshashai community. Newfoundland and Labrador. June 1997.

Queen Elizabeth II and The Duke of Edinburgh place a wreath at the Tomb of the Unknown Soldier at the base of the National War Memorial. Ottawa, Ontario. October 2002.

The presentation of a bouquet.
Edmonton, Alberta. May 2005

And as in all our visits down the years, whether watching a chuck wagon race at the Calgary Stampede or athletic prowess at the Montréal Olympics, whether listening to an Inuit song of greeting in Nunavut or the skirl of pipes in Nova Scotia, I have always felt not only welcome but at home in Canada. Of course the relationship between Crown and Canada evolves with the times – as it should. But I for one sense the continuity; it seems to me like yesterday that small girls offered me flowers on my first visit fifty four years ago. Yet today, I suspect, it is their grandchildren who are presenting the bouquets.

Queen Elizabeth II
Edmonton, Alberta
May 2005

God Save The Queen

God Save our gracious Queen!

Long live our noble Queen!

God save The Queen!

Send her victorious,

Happy and glorious,

Long to reign over us,

God save The Queen!

The Royal Anthem

The anthem originated as a patriotic song in London, England, in 1745. Neither the author nor the composer is known. Since the proclamation of "O Canada" as the National Anthem in 1980, "God Save The Queen" has been performed as the Royal Anthem of Canada in the presence of members of the Royal Family, as part of the Salute accorded to the Governor General and Lieutenant Governors and on other occasions.

APPENDICES

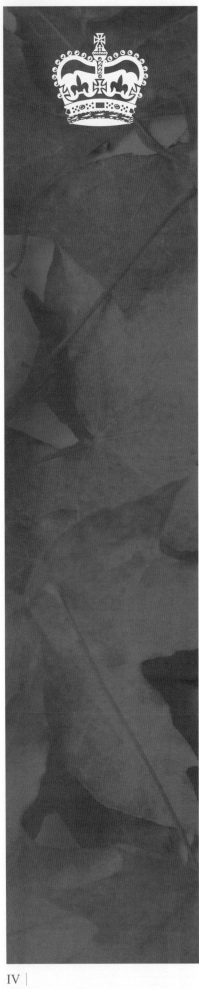

Sovereigns of Canada

1485 - 1509	Henry VII	1515 - 1547	François I
1509 - 1547	Henry VIII	1547 - 1559	Henri II
1547 - 1553	Edward VI	1559 - 1560	François II
1553 - 1558	Mary I	1560 - 1574	Charles IX
1558 - 1603	Elizabeth I	1574 - 1589	Henri III
1603 - 1625	James I	1589 - 1610	Henri IV
1625 - 1649	Charles I	1610 - 1643	Louis XIII
1649 - 1660	(Cromwellian Era)	1643 - 1715	Louis XIV
1660 - 1685	Charles II	1715 - 1775	Louis XV
1685 - 1688	James II		
1688 - 1702	William III		
1688 - 1694	and Mary II		
1702 - 1714	Anne		
1714 - 1727	George I		
1727 - 1760	George II		
1760 - 1820	George III		
1820 - 1830	George IV		
1830 - 1837	William IV		
1837 - 1901	Victoria		
1901 - 1910	Edward VII		
1910 - 1936	George V		
1936	Edward VIII		
1936 - 1952	George VI		
1952 -	Elizabeth II		

Governors / Governors General of Canada

1627 - 1635	Samuel de Champlain
1635 - 1648	Charles de Montmagny
1648 - 1651	Louis d'Ailleboust de Coulonge
1651 - 1657	Jean de Lauzon
1658 - 1661	Le vicomte d'Argenson
1661 - 1663	Le baron d'Avaugour
1663 - 1665	Augustin de Mésy
1665 - 1672	Daniel de Courcelle
1672 - 1682	Le comte de Frontenac
1689 - 1698	"
1682 - 1685	Joseph-Antoine de LaBarre
1685 - 1689	Le marquis de Denonville
1698 - 1703	Hector de Callière
1703 - 1725	Philippe de Vaudreuil
1726 - 1747	Le marquis de Beauharnois
1747 - 1749	Le comte de La Galissonnière
1749 - 1752	Le marquis de La Jonquière
1752 - 1755	Le marquis de Duquesne
1755 - 1760	Pierre de Vaudreuil
1760 - 1763	Jeffrey Amherst
1764 - 1768	James Murray
1768 - 1778	Sir Guy Carleton, Lord Dorchester
1786 - 1796	"
1778 - 1786	Frederick Haldimand
1796 - 1807	Robert Prescott
1807 - 1811	Sir James Craig
1812 - 1815	Sir George Prevost

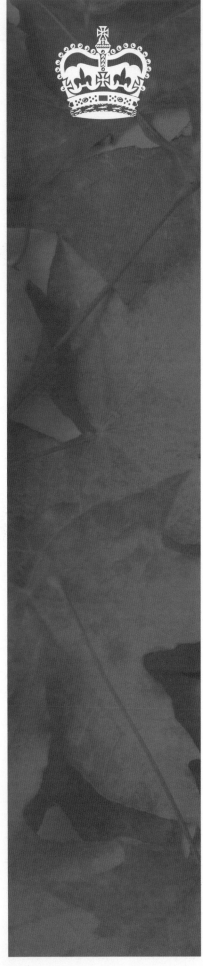

1816 - 1818	Sir John Sherbrooke
1818 - 1819	The Duke of Richmond
1820 - 1828	The Earl of Dalhousie
1830 - 1835	Lord Aylmer
1835 - 1838	The Earl of Gosford
1838	The Earl of Durham
1838 - 1839	Sir John Colborne
1839 - 1841	Lord Sydenham
1842 - 1843	Sir Charles Bagot
1843 - 1845	Lord Metcalfe
1845 - 1847	The Earl of Cathcart
1847 - 1854	The Earl of Elgin
1854 - 1861	Sir Edmund Head
1861 - 1868	Viscount Monck
1868 - 1872	Lord Lisgar
1872 - 1878	The Earl of Dufferin
1878 - 1883	The Marquess of Lorne
1883 - 1888	The Marquess of Lansdowne
1888 - 1893	Lord Stanley of Preston
1893 - 1898	The Earl of Aberdeen

1898 - 1904	The Earl of Minto
1904 - 1911	The Earl of Grey
1911 - 1916	Prince Arthur, Duke of Connaught
1916 - 1921	The Duke of Devonshire
1921 - 1926	Lord Byng of Vimy
1926 - 1931	Viscount Willingdon of Ratton
1931 - 1935	The Earl of Bessborough
1935 - 1940	Lord Tweedsmuir of Elsfeld
1940 - 1946	The Earl of Athlone
1946 - 1952	Viscount Alexander of Tunis
1952 - 1959	Vincent Massey
1959 - 1967	Georges-Philéas Vanier
1967 - 1974	Roland Michener
1974 - 1979	Jules Léger
1979 - 1984	Edward Schreyer
1984 - 1990	Jeanne Sauvé
1990 - 1995	Ramon John Hnatyshyn
1995 - 1999	Roméo LeBlanc
1999 - 2005	Adrienne Clarkson
2005 -	Michaëlle Jean

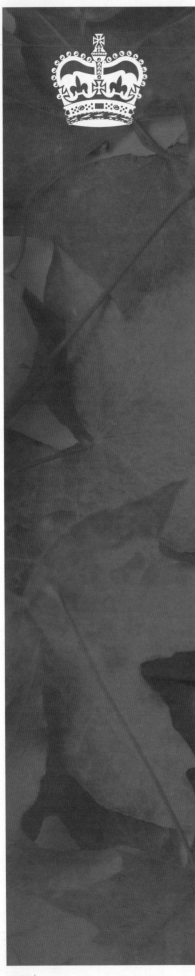

Photographic Credits

Unless otherwise specified, all photographs of Royal Visits are credited to the Department of Canadian Heritage (Victor Pilon, André Rozon, Denis Drever) while all photographs of the current and former Governors General are credited to Government House, Ottawa (Rideau Hall).

Introduction

The Queen and Prime Minister Harper – Office of the Prime Minister

Chapter 1

pg. 2 | The Royal Arms of Canada and Canadian Flag – Department of Canadian Heritage

pg. 3 | Princess Elizabeth dances at Rideau Hall; The Queen and Duke of Edinburgh with Governor General Massey – The National Archives of Canada

Chapter 2

pg. 6 | The Arms of Royalist France – The National Archives of Canada

pg. 6 | The Sovereign Council – Ministry of Communications, Province of Québec

pg. 7 | King Edward I of England – The Collection of Her Majesty The Queen

pg. 7 | King Louis IX of France – Attributed to Eustache le Sueur and donated by Albert Almon to the Collection of Cape Breton University Art Gallery (Photographer: Ruby Powell, Curatorial Collections Specialist, Fortress of Louisbourg)

pg. 8 | The Fathers of Confederation - Public Information Office, House of Commons, Ottawa, Ontario

pg. 8 | The Arms of the City of Québec – Government House, Ottawa (Rideau Hall)

pg. 8 | *The British North America Act, 1867* – Department of the Provincial Secretary, Province of Saskatchewan

pg. 9 | The Queen at Vimy Ridge – Office of the Prime Minister

pg. 9 | Lieutenant Governor Duchesne – Office of the Lieutenant Governor of Quebec

pg. 11 | Historic Flags of Canada – Department of Canadian Heritage

Chapter 3

pg. 16 | The Great Seal of Canada – Office of the Registrar General (Industry Canada)

pg. 17 | The Queen's Personal Canadian Flag – Department of Canadian Heritage

pg. 18 | Lieutenant Governor Hagerman – Office of the Lieutenant Governor of Prince Edward Island

pg. 18 | Royal Assent – Senate Communications, Ottawa, Ontario

pg. 19 | Lieutenant Governor Harvard – Office of the Lieutenant Governor of Manitoba

pg. 20 | Lieutenant Governor and Mrs. Barnhart – Office of the Lieutenant Governor of Saskatchewan

Chapter 4

pg. 24 | The Parliament Buildings – Industry Canada

pg. 25 | The Mace of the House of Commons – Industry Canada

pg. 25 | The House of Commons Chamber – Public Information Office, House of Commons, Ottawa, Ontario

pg. 25 | The Senate Chamber – Senate Communications, Ottawa, Ontario

pg. 26 | The Queen reads Speeches from Throne (1957, 1977) – National Archives of Canada

pg. 28 | The swearing in of Prime Minister Harper and Cabinet – Government House, Ottawa (Rideau Hall)

pg. 29 | The Queen's Golden Jubilee Flag – Department of Canadian Heritage

pg. 29 | The Coronation, Silver and Golden Jubilee Medals – Department of National Defence

pg. 29 | Brian Adams and Canada Post stamp – Government House, Ottawa (Rideau Hall)

pg. 31 | Lieutenant Governor and Mrs. Kwong – Office of the Lieutenant Governor of Alberta

Chapter 5

pg. 34 | The Governor General's Flag – Department of Canadian Heritage

pg. 34 | Government House, Ottawa – Government House, Ottawa (Rideau Hall)

pg. 34 | Samuel de Champlain – National Archives of Canada

pg. 37 | Lieutenant Governor McGibbon and Lieutenant Governor Alexander – Ministry of Government Services (Archives of Ontario), Province of Ontario

pg. 37 | Lieutenant Governor Steinhauer - Collection of the Government of Alberta. Reproduced by permission of the Speaker of the Legislative Assembly of Alberta.

pg. 38 | Lieutenant Governor Chiasson – Office of the Lieutenant Governor of New Brunswick

pg. 38 | Lieutenant Governor Francis – Office of the Lieutenant Governor of Nova Scotia

pg. 39 | Children await their Sovereign (1939) – National Archives of Canada

pg. 41 | Governor General Georges Vanier - Cavouk

pg. 41 | Badges of the Canadian Forces and the Royal 22nd Regiment – Department of National Defence

Chapter 6

pg. 44 | Canadian Flag in Washington and Canadian/American flags – Department of Foreign Affairs and International Trade (Canadian Embassy, Washington)

pg. 45 | Centre Block, Parliament Hill – Library of Parliament, Mone Cheng

pg. 46 | The Queen and Archbishop Tutu – The Commonwealth Secretariat, London

Chapter 7

pg. 50 | The Queen at RCMP Equitation Centre – Victor Pilon; Birthday stamp – Canada Post Corporation (photographer – Victor Pilon)

pg. 50 | The Queen Elizabeth Way highway sign – Ministry of Transportation, Government of Ontario

pg. 50 | Dollar coin – The Royal Canadian Mint

pg. 50 | Twenty dollar bill – The Bank of Canada

pg. 51 | Badges: Royal Canadian Mounted Police – RCMP; Ontario Provincial Police – OPP; Royal Newfoundland Constabulary – RNC; Canadian Security Intelligence Service – CSIS; Cape Breton Regional Police Service – CBRPS; Royal Canadian Legion – RCL; Vancouver Police Department – VPD

pg. 52 | Insignia of the Order of Canada – Government House, Ottawa (Rideau Hall)

pg. 52 | The Queen and Jules Léger – John Evans

pg. 52 | Nelson Mandela and the Order of Canada – The Canadian Press / Tom Hanson

pg. 52 | Order of Newfoundland and Labrador – Government of Newfoundland and Labrador; Order of Ontario - Government of Ontario; Order of British Columbia – Government of British Columbia

pg. 53 | Arms of the Canadian Heraldic Authority, Badge of the Siksika Nation and Presentation of Badge to the Siksika Nation – Government House, Ottawa (Rideau Hall)

pg. 53 | Presentation of *Letters Patent, 1988* – Government House, Ottawa (Rideau Hall)

pg. 54 | Governor General Schreyer accepts Parliamentary Address –The National Archives of Canada

pg. 55 | King George VI and Queen Elizabeth (1939) – The National Archives of Canada

pg. 56 | The Queen at the Canadian Light Source Synchrotron – André Rozon; Definitive stamp – Canada Post Corporation (photographer – André Rozon)

Chapter 8

pg. 61 | Royal Cypher – Department of Canadian Heritage

pg. 62 | Governor General Schreyer and Terry Fox – Ottawa Citizen / Wayne Cuttington

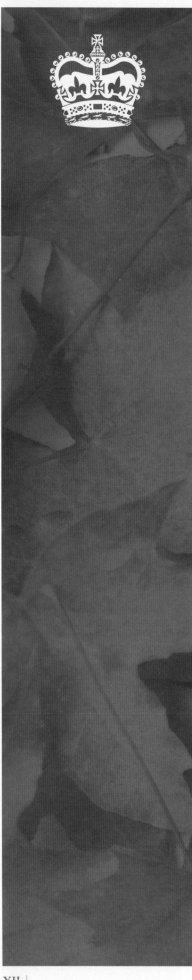

Glossary

Armorial bearings: Distinguishing symbols or designs used by nations, governments, corporations, institutions and individuals to indicate sovereignty, authority, ownership and identity. Also known as coats of arms.

British North America Act, 1867: A statute of the British Parliament in 1867 that provided for the creation of the Dominion of Canada. As Canada's original constitution (in 1982 renamed *Constitution Act, 1867*), it has been amended many times and, along with other legislative documents and decrees, forms an integral part of Canada's Constitution.

Canadian Crown: All executive powers exercised by or on behalf of Her Majesty Queen Elizabeth II, as Queen of Canada, within our system of constitutional monarchy, which ensures effective and orderly government.

Collective Crown: A term used to describe the institution comprised of the Sovereign (Queen Elizabeth II as Queen of Canada) and her eleven direct representatives: the Governor General (federal jurisdiction) and the ten Lieutenant Governors (provincial jurisdictions).

Commonwealth: A free association of 53 nations from around the world that were once colonies of Great Britain. All nations are equal partners, dedicated to cooperation in the interest of freedom and development, and recognize the Queen as Head of the Commonwealth.

Confederation: The union of Upper Canada (Ontario), Lower Canada (Québec), Nova Scotia and New Brunswick as provided for by the *British North America Act, 1867* to form the Dominion of Canada.

Congressional democracy: A system of government in which there is a clear separation between the executive (President and Cabinet) and legislative (Congress) branches of government. The executive branch is not directly accountable to the legislative, which is made up of the elected representatives of the people.

Constitution Act, 1867: See *British North America Act, 1867*.

Constitutional convention: Well-established customs or practices, which have evolved over time and are integral aspects of our system of government even though they are not specifically mentioned in the Constitution. One of three elements that make up Canada's Constitution: written constitution, legislation, and unwritten constitution (rules of common law and conventions).

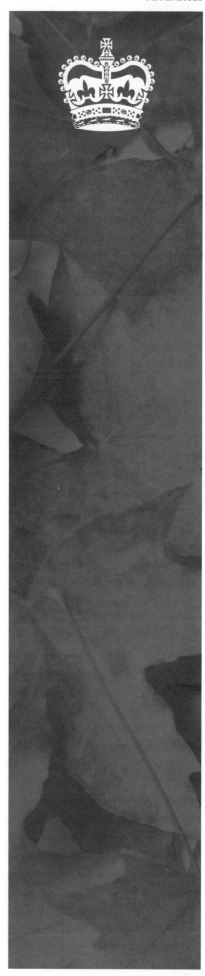

Constitutional monarchy: A form of government in which executive powers (Crown) are exercised by or on behalf of the Sovereign and on the basis of ministerial advice.

Court of Queen's Bench: The superior-court trial division in the provincial jurisdiction (New Brunswick, Manitoba, Saskatchewan and Alberta). Different names are used in other provinces and territories (Nova Scotia, British Columbia, Prince Edward Island, Newfoundland, Northwest Territories, Yukon and Nunavut: "Supreme Court"; Québec: "Superior Court"; Ontario: "Ontario Court, General Division").

Crown of Canada: See Canadian Crown.

Crown land: Land belonging to the government, whether in the national or provincial jurisdiction.

Crown corporations: Corporations in which the government, be it at the national or provincial level, has total or majority ownership. Organized on the pattern of private enterprises, they have a mandate to provide specific goods and/or services.

Decorations for Bravery: Honours awarded to people who have incurred a grave risk of injury or have placed their lives in jeopardy in attempting to rescue others. These honours are awarded by the Governor General on behalf of the Queen.

Dissolution of Parliament: The termination of the life of a Parliament, and by extension the ruling government, which is followed by a general election. Dissolution is proclaimed by the representative of the Queen on the advice of the Prime Minister or Premier.

Equerry: An officer of the Canadian Forces appointed to attend the Queen or a member of the Royal Family during a visit to Canada.

Executive: The branch of government that carries out the law — the cabinet and ruling government that sit in the elected chamber (House of Commons/Legislature). Also referred to as "The Queen in Council."

Executive Council: The Premier of the province and members of the cabinet, which are akin to the Privy Council (Prime Minister and members of the cabinet) in the federal jurisdiction.

Fathers of Confederation: The 36 delegates who, between 1864 and 1867, met to discuss terms of union for the British North American colonies that led to the creation of the Dominion of Canada in 1867.

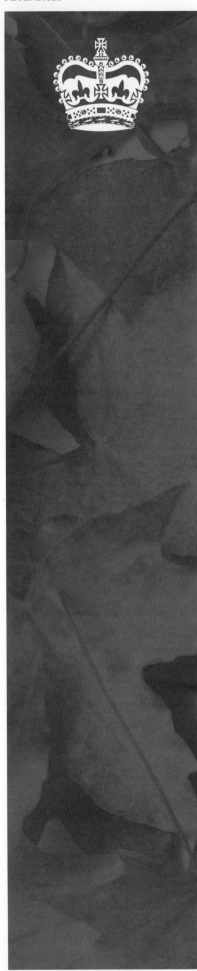

Federal state: A nation that brings together different political communities with a national government for common purposes and separate (provincial/state) governments for the particular purposes of each community.

Government House: Her Majesty's official residences in Canada, situated in Ottawa and most provincial capitals and occupied by the Queen's representative. Government House in Ottawa is known as Rideau Hall.

Governor: The personal representative of the French king who directed operations in New France on behalf of the French Crown; this function was in effect from 1627 until 1760. Subsequently, governors served as colonial administrators under the British Crown.

Governor General: The personal representative of the Queen who acts on her behalf in performing certain duties and responsibilities in the federal jurisdiction.

House of Commons: The elected, lower chamber of Canada's parliament through which all legislation must pass before it becomes law. The members are chosen in general elections held every four years based on fixed election dates, pursuant to new legislation passed in 2007.

Judicial: The branch of government that interprets the law — in other words, the courts. Also referred to as "The Queen in Banco" or "The Queen on the Bench."

Legislative: The branch of government that makes the laws — Parliament of Canada/provincial and territorial legislatures. Also referred to as "The Queen in Parliament."

Legislature: The federal legislature (Parliament of Canada) consists of the Queen, the Senate, and the House of Commons. The provincial legislatures consist of the Lieutenant Governor and the elected house.

Letters of Credence: Formal letters accrediting Canadian ambassadors/particular high commissioners as the official representatives of Canada in foreign states.

Letters Patent: A document issued by the Sovereign that serves as an instrument of conveyance or grant, in areas as diverse as land, franchises and offices. The Letters Patent issued by King George VI in 1947 transferred most of the Sovereign's powers to the Governor General to be exercised in Canada.

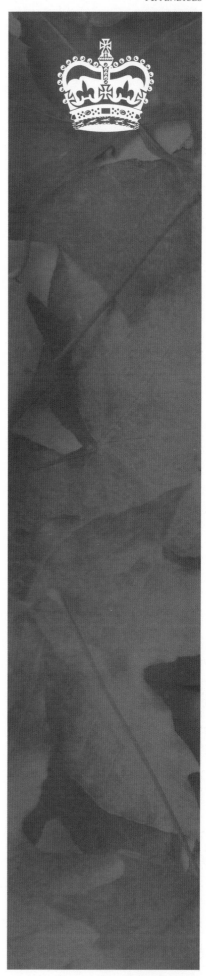

Lieutenant Governor: The personal representative of the Queen who acts on her behalf in performing certain duties and responsibilities in the provincial jurisdiction.

Mace: A staff, normally bearing a Crown, that rests in Canadian legislative chambers while the chambers are in session. The mace symbolizes the legitimate right of the legislatures to sit under authority of the Crown.

Magna Carta: The charter of English personal and political liberties granted by King John at Runnymede, England, in 1215.

Majority government: A government formed by the leader of the political party who has won a majority of seats in the House of Commons/legislature following a general election.

Meritorious Service Decorations (Military and Civil Decorations): Honours awarded to Canadians or non-Canadians for a deed or activity performed in a professional manner or of a high standard that brings benefit or honour to the Canadian Forces or to Canada. These honours are awarded by the Governor General on behalf of the Queen.

Ministers of the Crown: Members of a government who are selected by the Prime Minister/Premier to be given cabinet responsibilities in specific areas and to be known as cabinet ministers. The oath of office is administered in the presence of the Sovereign's representative.

Minority government: A government formed when no party holds a clear majority of seats in the House of Commons/legislature following a general election. Usually, the government is formed by the party with the most seats.

Order of Military Merit: Honours awarded to regular or reserve members of the Canadian Forces to recognize conspicuous merit and exceptional service. These honours are awarded by the Governor General on behalf of the Queen.

Order of Canada: Honours awarded to Canadians to recognize their achievement in important fields of human endeavour and service to their country. These honours are awarded by the Governor General on behalf of the Queen.

Parliament of Canada: The supreme legislature of Canada consisting of the Queen (represented by the Governor General), the Senate and the House of Commons.

Parliamentary democracy: A British system of government in which the executive (Prime Minister/Premier and cabinet) sit in the elected chamber (House of Commons/Legislature) and are accountable to the elected representatives of the people. From time to time, members of the Executive (Ministers of the Crown) have sat in the upper chamber (the Senate).

Patriation of the Constitution: The 1982 process whereby the British Parliament divested itself of its power to amend the Canadian Constitution, and the *Constitution Act, 1982* provided Canada with its own amending formula.

Premier: The first minister, or head, of a provincial government, who is also the leader of the party in power.

Prerogative powers: Those powers of the Crown that are based in constitutional convention — discretionary authority exercised by the Crown. See also Royal prerogative.

Prime Minister: The first minister, or head, of a federal government, who is also the leader of the party in power.

Privy Council: The Prime Minister and members of the cabinet — the equivalent of the Executive Council (Premier and members of the cabinet) in the provincial jurisdiction.

Republic: A nation with an elected or nominated president who may serve as both head of government and head of state or simply as head of state.

Reserve powers: Powers that remain vested in the Crown that can be used by the Queen and her representatives (Governor General and Lieutenant Governors) in special situations.

Responsible government: A government that is responsible to the people, based on the principle that governments must be responsible to the representatives of the people.

Royal Assent: The consent granted by the Queen's representative (Governor General or Lieutenant Governor), which serves as the Crown's approval of a bill, thereby making it an act (law).

Royal Prerogative: The historic rights and privileges from which flow all executive powers (the Crown) as exercised by the Sovereign.

Royal commissions: Official inquiries into matters of public concern that have their historic origin with the Sovereign's prerogative powers to order investigations.

Senate: The appointed, upper chamber of Canada's parliament through which all legislation must pass before it becomes law.

Sovereign: The king or queen; the ruling monarch.

Speech from the Throne: A statement of work being proposed by the government to be undertaken in the parliamentary session being opened. The speech is prepared by the government and read by the Governor General or the Lieutenant Governor. In Québec, the Speech from the Throne is read by the Premier in the presence of the Lieutenant Governor.

Statute of Westminster, 1931: A law of the British Parliament (December 11, 1931) that granted Canada and other dominions full legal independence and legislative autonomy, thus ending Britain's overriding authority over Dominion legislation.

Statutory powers: Powers that are written in law.

Victoria Day: A national holiday established by Parliament in 1901 and observed on the first Monday preceding May 25. Originally intended to honour the birthday of Queen Victoria, the day now celebrates the birthday of Queen Elizabeth II (although the actual date is April 21).

Vote of non-confidence: A vote on a motion that indicates that the government has lost the confidence of the House if it is adopted. The government would then normally resign or request the Governor General/Lieutenant Governor to dissolve Parliament/Legislature and issue election writs.

Acknowledgements

The Department of Canadian Heritage wishes to extend sincere gratitude and thanks to the following:

Kevin S. MacLeod, C.V.O.

Chief of Protocol, Department of Canadian Heritage

Author

Dr. D. Michael Jackson, C.V.O., S.O.M., C.D.

&

Father Jacques Monet, S.J., F.R.S.C.

Advisors on Text

Creative Edge Communications (Ottawa)

Editorial Services

VC One Communications Inc. (Ottawa)

Artistic Design and Graphic Layout Services

Numerous partners in the private and public sectors

Use of Graphics / Photography